BASEBALL
A CELEBRATION!

JAMES BUCKLEY, JR. & JIM GIGLIOTTI

MAJOR LEAGUE BASEBALL™

BASEBALL
A CELEBRATION!

IN ASSOCIATION WITH **MAJOR LEAGUE BASEBALL**

JAMES BUCKLEY, JR. & JIM GIGLIOTTI

DK

LONDON, NEW YORK, DELHI, SYDNEY,
MUNICH, PARIS and JOHANNESBURG

London, New York, Sydney, Delhi,
Paris, Munich and Johannesburg

Book Designer: Diana Catherines
Art Editor: Megan Clayton
Project Editor: Crystal A. Coble
Jacket Designers: Dirk Kaufman and Megan Clayton
Editorial Director: Chuck Wills
Art Director: Tina Vaughan
Publisher: Sean Moore
Production Manager: Chris Avgherinos
Picture Research: Shoreline Publishing Group

MAJOR LEAGUE BASEBALL

Timothy J. Brosnan, Executive Vice President, Business
Don Hintze, Vice President, Publishing
Rich Pilling, Manager, MLB Photos
Paul Cunningham, Photo Editor
Mike McCormack, Editor
Erin Whiteside, Assistant Editor

Major League Baseball Properties, Inc.
245 Park Avenue, New York, NY 10167

First American Edition, 2001
2 4 6 8 10 9 7 5 3 1
Published in the United States
by DK Publishing, Inc.
95 Madison Avenue, New York, New York 10016

DK Publishing, Inc. offers special discounts for bulk purchases for sales promotions or premiums.
Specific, large-quantity needs can be met with special editions, including personalized covers,
excerpts of existing guides, and corporate imprints. For more information, contact Special Markets Department,
DK Publishing, Inc.,95 Madison Avenue, New York, NY 10016 Fax: 800-600-9098.

Library of Congress Cataloging-in-Publication Data
Buckley, James, Jr.
  Baseball, a celebration! / James Buckley, Jr., Jim Gigliotti.
    p. cm.
  ISBN 0-7894-8018-2 (alk. paper)
  1. Baseball--United States--History. 2. Baseball--United
States--History--Pictorial works.   I. Title: Baseball. II. Gigliotti,
Jim. III. Title.
  GV863.A1 B83 2001
  796.357'0973--dc21
                          2001032454

Reproduced by Colourscan, Singapore
Printed and bound in Germany by Mohndruck GmbH

See our complete catalog at
www.dk.com

Contents

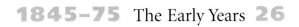

Introduction

By James Buckley, Jr.

(*left*) Bob Feller fires a pitch toward a waiting Joe DiMaggio; (*above*) The author's great-grandfather Nick Minden (upper left) and his 1922 team.

MY GREAT-GRANDFATHER RAN A BASEBALL team back in 1922. That's him in the picture above, at the left end of the back row, wearing the hat and tie, standing behind the Charleston, Arkansas, team that he and his lumber yard sponsored.

In 1946, my grandfather (on my father's side) had one ticket to a World Series game between the Boston Red Sox and the St. Louis Cardinals. Instead of using it for himself, instead of seeing his beloved Sox play in their first Series since 1918, he gave the prized ticket to my father, who was 14 at the time.

In 1972, my father took me to my first baseball game. It was played at Fenway Park, the same place he had seen that Series game in '46. We watched the Sox beat the Athletics 9-2, and there in front of my eyes for the very first time, I saw my hero, Carl Yastrzemski.

In 1979, I kept a daily count of Yaz's stats on yellow legal pads, as he marched toward career totals of 3,000 hits and 400 home runs. Before school each morning, I checked the box scores and marked off another step on the road we were traveling together.

In 2001, my son Conor, who is three, can watch a game on TV and tell you which guy is the batter, which

October 4, 1967: Yaz, though a Triple Crown winner, took extra batting practice following the Red Sox Game 1 loss to the Cardinals in the World Series.

guy is the pitcher, and which guy is the umpire. Ask him his favorite team, and he'll tell you the same one his own great-grandfather loved, the same one his grandfather followed, and the one his father aches for annually: The Boston Red Sox.

The point of this little family history is not to brag (obviously, since the Sox finished the 20th century on an 80-plus-year championship-less streak), but rather to show that the great thing about baseball is that any American reading this could probably, unless they've just arrived here from Mars, recite a strikingly similar tale about his or her family and the game. The team might be different, the locations of the games or the memories might vary, it might be the Majors, the

minors, or a high school team, but there would always be baseball. For more than 150 years, there has always been baseball. It has changed, it has evolved, it has added sad moments to its glorious history, it has created moments of immortal joy. But it has always been there, for every generation.

This book celebrates in photographs not only the passing of time from baseball's earliest days to its colorful present, but the passing of the story of baseball from one generation to the next. The game of baseball as myth-song of American history is a cliche as old as Jack Armstrong and Frank Merriwell, All-American Boys, as prevalent in baseball poetry as the metaphor of spring, as well-known as the final

2000: A Santa Barbara, California, player practices taking grounders. He joins millions of kids who dream the Major League dream of generations past.

scene of *Field of Dreams*, when Kevin Costner plays catch with his long-dead father.

But all cliches, no matter how hoary, have real roots; they spring from established truths. The cliche of baseball being the solid, unbroken line that traces well more than half of the history of this nation is all the more true for its ubiquity in literature. The game really can be seen to define a nation.

It grew up in innocence, a game played by people in the open fields that still stood near cities and towns. It spread through a nation riven with war that stopped once in a while to play a game; a well-known painting from 1863 shows Union Army soldiers playing a game at a Confederate prison camp.

It suffered through adolescence, growing from game to business, even as America grew from agrarian republic to world-dominating economic and industrial power. It, like America, survived world wars . . . at least twice . . . and grew stronger for the survival.

It suffered from the mounting distractions of modern life as the end of the 20th century came closer, but has recovered to reach heights of popularity and prosperity it has never known before.

Baseball has gone through all those things, and we, the fans, have gone right along with it.

In this book, the medium for telling this story is photography. There are no drawings, no paintings . . . all these images are of real human beings engaged in the sport. The main prism for the view we take of baseball is from the professional level on down. The focus is Major League Baseball, the top echelon of play and the main focus of most fans. Yet as the game touches the nation in so many ways, so, too, do the photographs touch many of game's different faces, from young people playing Little League or sandlot ball in knickers to a game played on ice in Antarctica. The game touches the world, too, more and more each year, and baseball's growing international reach is reflected in this book.

Baseball: A Celebration is by no means a complete record of the photographic history of baseball. Creating such an all-encompassing record would have filled 10 volumes this size.

1942: Satchel Paige, looking forward, never back.

Rather, we see this collection as touching first, second, and third as we round toward home, toward the future, rather than examining each and every footstep as we race around the bases. So while your favorite player may not be in here, know that in fact he is, his era is, his game is, his life is. If he–or you–played the game, you will find a picture that will make your game come to life again, be it a memory of vision or experience.

As you make the journey, go slowly. Look around. Look past the uniforms, the bats, the gloves. Look at the moments in history, at the people and the emotion these pictures capture forever.

In the eyes of King Kelly (page 49), see a man who has heard a nation cheer for him; in the Byronic face of Addie Joss (page 85), see a life that will end before its time. In the photo of Honus Wagner (page 13), look back on a simpler time, before batting gloves, before millionaires, to an era when, for men like Wagner, it might be baseball or the mines.

In the crowds of kids surrounding an aging Babe Ruth (page 258), see more than their faces . . . see their joy. In the boyish glee of Ted Williams (page 234), share a love for the game few others ever have matched. In the champagne-soaked shout of Willie Mays (page 25), hear the sound of victory remembered by generations of winners. And in the titanic swing of Mark McGwire (page 584), relive the home-run chase that enthralled a nation in 1998.

There is emotion galore: Cheer with Giants fans as they joyously watch Bobby Thomson's "Shot Heard Round the World" leave the Polo Grounds in 1951. Cry with the world when Roberto Clemente was lost forever in 1972.

Celebrate with all of baseball moments from recent

1946: Art or photography? Or both? Stan Musial is caught in a rundown in 1946 and all three players are caught in a ballet-with-shadow.

years that capture the sweep of the game's history: Cal Ripken's streak-breaker, McGwire and Sammy Sosa's home run race, the gathering of greats for the All-Century Team, and many more.

Every baseball fan has a moment, captured in black-and-white or color, that calls to mind everything the game is, was, or could be. For me, that is captured in a photo that has hung on my wall for years and is reproduced here on page 10. The subject is Yastrzemski, my hero, but feel free to substitute your own hero and your own best-remembered image in this story. The

photograph was taken on October 4, 1967. The Red Sox, after winning one of the tightest pennant races in history–largely on the strength of Yastrzemski's Triple Crown season–had lost Game 1 of the 1967 World Series to St. Louis, 2-1. If you squint, you can just see the "St. Louis" and "Boston" on the Green Monster in the distance, and some red, white, and blue bunting at the base of the left-field seats.

The scene is well after the game is over, long after the fans have left. The player who had literally carried his team to the championship, who had been the best batter and slugger in the American League, had gone hitless in that Game 1 loss. This was unacceptable to him. Still sweaty from his Game 1 play, having suffered through the postgame grilling and after-action second-guessing by reporters, Yaz called for the batting cages to be rolled back out onto the field.

His bright red number 8 can be seen on his back as he finishes another swing, in the batting cage, after the game. I do not exaggerate when I say that sometimes when I think I've done well enough, sometimes when I think that my work is acceptable, when I think that "just enough" is indeed enough, sometimes when that happens, I look at that picture, and I go back to the well, back to the cage for a few more swings.

Think of that: Yaz took BP *after* that World Series game . . . and the next day, he went 3-for-4 with 4 RBI and had the first two of his three homers for the Series; the Red Sox won Game 2, 5-0.

Like a baseball team, this book was created through the efforts of many people. We especially send our eternal thanks to the many, many photographers, known and unknown, whose work graces this book. Without them, this book would be a pamphlet.

A word about the selection process for photographs in this book. It would have been simply impossible without the outstanding contributions of Paul Cunningham and Rich Pilling of Major League Baseball's photography department. Not only did they provide most of the more recent photographs in this book from MLB's own library, they also spent many days at the Baseball Hall of Fame and Library in Cooperstown, New York, poring through history to find the photos that would tell the story. Thanks to Bill Burdick of that outstanding organization in bucolic Cooperstown for his invaluable help as well.

It was my pleasure to handle the research from all other sources, and that was a trip in itself.

From MLB, from the Hall of Fame . . . from libraries, historical societies, private collections, freelance photographers, and established photo agencies (notably AP/Wide World and Corbis) . . . the photos poured in. They were assembled to tell the story in somewhat chronological fashion, trying to hit all the high points while making sure to include the grace notes.

My writing partner, Jim Gigliotti, and I tried to add some context, some information beyond the frame, that would carry the story along even further.

Throughout the months of photo-tripping through history, I lost count of how many times I bragged to friends who would ask what I was doing at "work."

"Looking at baseball photographs," I would crow. Nice work if you can get it.

Thanks, Great-grandpa Nick.
Thanks, Grandpa Francis.
Thanks, Dad.
Thanks, baseball.

—James Buckley, Jr.
Santa Barbara, California
April, 2001

Baseball Photography

By Jim Gigliotti

(left) Photographer Rich Pilling and the Twins' Dan Gladden caught Braves' catcher Greg Olson head over heels in the 1991 World Series.
(above) The 1988 Dodgers exult at the moment of triumph, as photographed by Jayne Kamin-Oncea.

WHEN STEVE HOWE CLOSED OUT THE Dodgers' 9-2 victory over the Yankees in Game 6 of the 1981 World Series, photographer Jayne Kamin-Oncea was there to capture the moment.

Kamin-Oncea got a joyous shot of the three Steves–Howe, first baseman Steve Garvey, and catcher Steve Yeager–celebrating on the infield. In the locker room, there were hugs and champagne spray all around, and Kamin-Oncea photographed much of the drama.

But she missed the one shot she really wanted.

"I wanted to capture the emotion from the dugout just as they won it," she says. "So I told myself that the next time I would be ready with a remote."

She had to wait until 1988. After the Dodgers built a 3-1 lead over the Oakland A's in the World Series, Kamin-Oncea was prepared for the celebration following Los Angeles's 5-2 win in Oakland in Game 5.

"I had a remote with a foot switch focused on the dugout," she says. "I shot the mound, as usual, but this time I also got them coming out of the dugout."

The result was a memorable photo of the Dodgers as they claimed the franchise's sixth world title.

You'll find the photograph on the previous page. It's one of hundreds of shots that help illustrate the glorious history of baseball, from an unknown photographer's depiction of the New York Baseball Club from 1855 on page 30 (the Society for American Baseball Research calls this the oldest known baseball photograph) to a tender embrace between Barry Bonds and his father, Bobby, in 2001 on page 623–and a whole lot in between.

It was in 1839 that Louis Jacques Mandé Daguerre and officials in France officially announced the invention of photography. Kamin-Oncea's remote could hardly have been envisioned by Daguerre when he was credited with inventing photography. Nor could today's lightning-fast shutter speeds, nearly instant global transmission, or digital photography.

Abner Doubleday is often credited with inventing baseball in Cooperstown, New York, that same year.

There's as much fiction as fact in the two events. Daguerre hardly was alone in the development of photography. And there is no evidence that Cooperstown was the birthplace of baseball or Doubleday its father.

But no matter their true origins, baseball and photography fit each other as snugly as ball and glove, and their marriage was destined from the start. They grew up together in the 1800s, matured through growing innovation and technology, and emerged as viable professions and hobbies.

At first, it hardly seemed likely that the two arts would cross. It not only took a while for photographers to turn their attention to something as "trivial" as baseball, but the earliest forms of photography could

The Brooklyn Excelsiors, one of the best of the early amateur teams, pose for a photograph in 1859.

not capture the action of a pitcher in his windup or a player swinging a bat, let alone someone sliding into home.

But photography evolved quickly, with each new process helping to bring photography out of the portrait studio. In the 1860s, Matthew Brady and others brought graphic images of Civil War battlefields to the public.

In 1869, Brady shot a studio portrait of the Cincinnati Red Stockings (page 35), baseball's first professional team. Still, few photographers were willing to bring the camera out to the park. For one thing, cameras were still generally big and bulky and had to be lugged around the field, and shutter speeds were too slow for generating anything but posed pictures.

But then, a succession of events helped bring the camera to the park. In the late nineteenth century, Kodak's portable camera brought photography to the masses and stimulated interest again, and halftone plates made it feasible to put photographs in newspapers.

A vintage player and a vintage photograph: Ty Cobb rounding third.

And in 1904, John B. Foster, the editor of *Spalding's Official Baseball Guide*, approached Charles M. Conlon, a proofreader from the *New York Telegram.* Foster knew that Conlon's hobby was taking pictures.

"Charley, they need pictures of ball players for the *Guide*," Foster said. "There is no reason you can't take pictures of players, as well as pictures of landscapes."

"No man ever did a bigger favor than John B. Foster did for me that morning in 1904," Conlon wrote in *The Sporting News* more than three decades later.

And no photographer ever did a bigger favor for baseball. Conlon shot baseball games and players until 1942. His prolific work, some of which you'll find in this book, appeared annually in the *Spalding Guide, The Sporting News,* the *Telegram* (eventually the *World-Telegram*), and on various trading cards and promotional materials.

With shots from Conlon and others appearing daily in the newspapers, photographers became more of a presence at the field. And the range of pictures they could take was almost unlimited because their movement was not restricted.

Except for between the lines, photographers could go just about anywhere, and sometimes positioned themselves just a few feet from the batter. Note the photo of Joe DiMaggio on the next page, a situation which would be unthinkable today.

"Don't I wish I could have worked on the field like that!" says Rich Pilling, Major League Baseball's director of photography.

"Imagine being down there when Mark McGwire or Sammy Sosa belted a home run," veteran photographer Al Messerschmidt says.

Such photographer access in the early to mid-twentieth century meant some dramatic shots–but it wasn't without its hazards, as well.

Conlon wrote that he had seen camermen get hurt badly, but he got hurt only once, when John Titus of the Philadelphia Phillies struck him with a line drive early in the photographer's career. "It still hurts," Conlon said more than a quarter century later.

As late as 1974, when Pilling first began shooting major-league games, photographers still were allowed to work from the warning track in foul territory in a few cities.

"I got hit by screaming foul balls, and quickly learned that you have to watch where the action is," Pilling says. "You couldn't watch the ball, you had to watch the players coming your way and know when you had to get out of the area."

Today's photographers generally are stationed near the dugouts and are less likely to get in harm's way. Still, what they gain in safety, they lose in creativity.

"In the past, you could pick the angle and fine-tune it," Pilling says, "as opposed to being situated in a camera well."

No one loved Babe Ruth more than kids, and Babe returned their love in Ruthian style. This photo is from 1927.

Of course, not even the camera well is totally safe.

Messerschmidt, a resident of Florida who shoots Marlins games and Grapefruit League spring training action for a number of teams, was in Oakland in the late 1980s when Athletics first baseman Mark McGwire came racing toward the camera well while chasing a foul pop.

Messerschmidt managed to elude the hulking McGwire, as well as the ball–but his camera was not so lucky. The first baseman stopped near the railing of the well, but didn't reach in for the ball.

"It came straight down on the end of my lens hood, and put a great, big dent in it," Messerschmidt says.

Even as camera wells and restrictions have taken photographers further from the action in one sense, equipment changes have brought photographers even closer in another sense.

"From the days of the four-by-five-speed cameras looking over the umpire's shoulder, photographers have been pushed further and further from the action," Messerschmidt says. "But now we have longer and faster lenses and higher-speed motors."

Today's technology even gives the average fan in the stands the resources to shoot photographs which will make their memories last a lifetime.

"The auto-focus cameras make people photographers, and they make good photographers even better," Pilling says. "Still, the new cameras are just a tool. Photography is something you have to learn and work at. You can't just rely on technology."

While familiarity with equipment and the fundamentals of photography are essential to any baseball photographer, the refrain that comes up most is a knowledge of the game.

Photographers are part of the action with Joe DiMaggio in a game in 1938.

"Shooting baseball is more of a challenge than shooting other sports," Pilling says. "You really have to work at it to find the right shot. You have to anticipate the action."

To Messerschmidt, that means that, "if a situation calls for a potential squeeze or a double play and you don't know it, you might not be set up for it and you might miss it."

"Knowing the players helps, too," says Al Ainspan, the director of photography for Fleer Trading Cards. "A few years ago, we used a photograph of Jose Canseco making a snow-cone catch in the outfield." Canseco was not exactly known for stalwart defense, of course.

Trading cards have been a baseball staple for more than a century. Early photography on cards often included hokey attempts to simulate the game action that the technology of the era did not allow—for

example, placing a ball on a string in front of a batter or catcher.

Later, a photographer could shoot an entire team's worth of cards in one day before a game. But the hurried efforts did not produce realistic action, and sometimes resulted in errors or pranks, such as right-handed pitcher Lew Burdette posing as a southpaw in the 1950s, or the infamous expletive on the knob of Bill Ripken's bat in the 1980s.

Photo quality left something to be desired, too. Images were printed on the cardboard that came wrapped in waxy paper and accompanied by a rock-hard stick of gum. Today's cards feature excellent reproductions on high-quality paper. And with many players included in multiple sets, subsets, and insert cards, more and better photography is a necessity. Sammy Sosa, for instance, is a power hitter, but Ainspan will include photographs of him running the bases, sliding, or fielding.

"I also like to add interesting shots," Ainspan says. "Players signing autographs, laughing, smiling. I like to really bring out a player's personality."

For all photographers, that's always been easier with some players than with others.

Hall of Fame pitcher Rube Marquard once had Conlon hand over his photographic plate after the pitcher was photographed during warmups—for fear that the photo would somehow give away some secret to opponents. Lefty Grove never would pose with the ball in his hand.

But most players were happy to oblige Conlon, as well as current photographers.

"Players like Cal Ripken and Derek Jeter are the nicest guys in the world," Messerschmidt says. "Pedro Martinez is a great guy, very funny."

One hot afternoon in Fenway Park, Messerschmidt caught Martinez on film clowning around in the

(above) Lou Gehrig. *(right)* Willie Mays gets a champagne shower in 1973.

dugout. Martinez disappeared for a few minutes, then came back with some bottles of water, one of which he handed to the sweltering picture taker.

Kamin-Oncea generally liked to take up her spot in the camera well on the third-base side of Dodger Stadium, next to the home-team dugout.

"Steve Garvey had a habit of wiping the pine tar on his bat in the corner of the dugout," she says. "He did that one night and I gave him a thumbs-up. He gave me a little wave back with his pinkie, then went out and hit a home run. So every time I was there, he would scrape his bat in the corner and we'd exchange our signs. It was a good-luck thing."

Kamin-Oncea began shooting Dodgers games for the *Los Angeles Times* in her early twenties and would go out even on her off days. "I just really loved what I was doing," she says.

And that's another common denominator that separates the good baseball photographer from the rest: a passion for the profession.

"That's true for any top photographer," says Pilling, who still shoots about 80 games a year. "It will reflect in your work. I put my entire body and soul into my photographs. They are an extension of me. That's a cliche, I know, but it's true. When I'm at an event, sure, I'm looking through a camera lens, but I'm not–I'm part of the game."

Conlon, who died in 1945, never made his living from photography.

"But the fun I have had, the days in the open, the associations, the friendships, the confidences I have enjoyed . . . well, you can't buy those things," he wrote.

Messerschmidt enjoys shooting the old stadiums such as Wrigley Field and Fenway Park, but also likes to photograph college and minor-league baseball.

"They're all bright-eyed and dreaming about making

Then: Photographers (*opposite page*) stake out their positions at the old Polo Grounds in New York. Now: Photographers are further away, but closer than ever, to players (*above*).

the big leagues," he says. "The odds are slim, but they're out there trying."

Pilling speaks for baseball photographers everywhere, as well as legions of fans who have enjoyed baseball from its inception.

"Baseball is played outside, in the sunshine. It's in the summer. I love photographing it."

–Jim Gigliotti

1845-75

1845-75
The Early Years

1865 A common game
By the end of the Civil War, baseball was a nationwide pastime. Here (*previous pages*) players enjoy a game on Boston Common near houses that look much the same today.

c. 1860
James Creighton (*left*) was one of the game's early stars, as both a pitcher and hitter, and several Brooklyn clubs competed for his services. He died tragically at 21 of an injury received while hitting a home run.

c. 1848 and c. 1870
Alexander Cartwright was among the game's first pioneers; this photo (*above left*) is from later in his life. Writer Henry Chadwick (*above right*) helped champion the sport to the public and became its most tireless promoter and reporter.

It's fitting that the first real home of the game of baseball, a game that has been heaven-sent for millions of fans and generations of players, was at a place in New Jersey called the Elysian Fields.

What's also fitting is that for many years, the actual origin of a game that would create lasting legends was itself shrouded in myth.

The facts are these: Beginning in the 1840s, baseball was not so much born as it was evolved from numerous ball-and-stick games of centuries past, notably the English games of cricket and rounders. In typical American fashion, athletes in the U.S. adapted these games for their own.

The main driving force in early baseball was the Knickerbocker Base Ball (note the early spelling) Club of New York, founded in 1845. Led by Alexander Cartwright and Daniel Adams, the club tried many experiments before arriving at the basics of baseball, rules and practices which have survived nearly intact for more than 150 years.

The Knickerbockers played most of their games among themselves or against other local clubs, at the Elysian Fields in Hoboken, New Jersey. Their first official match was on June 19, 1846; they lost to the New York Base Ball Club 23-1.

The rest is history.

What is also a part of baseball history, but is now known to be far from the truth, is what is called the "Doubleday Myth."

In the early 1900s, player, promoter, and sporting goods magnate Albert Spalding began a campaign to identify the inventor of baseball. He came up with the story of how Union Army General Abner Doubleday had allegedly invented the sport in 1839 in Cooperstown, New York. The trouble was, Doubleday had never been there, and probably never saw a game in his life. But the myth persisted. For decades, Spalding's "inventor" took credit for the work of Cartwright and his club.

c. 1855 Oldest photo?
There is dispute over what is the
oldest photo of a team. One
contender is this 1855 or 1856 photo
(*top*) of the Gotham Base Ball Club.

c. 1860s Down on the farm
Not every team in baseball's early
days played in the big city. This club
(*bottom*), though not identified,
looks like one from a smaller town.

c. 1850s A base ball original
Here is the clubhouse of the
Philadelphia Base Ball Club
(*above*), founded in 1840 and
perhaps the oldest example of
sportsmen forming organizations
to play games of bat and ball.
Along with the Knickerbocker
and Gotham Clubs in New York,
teams were also formed in
Massachusetts, Pennsylvania,
and New Jersey.

1865 Hyperbole in action
There were few teams in the
Northeast, let alone the rest of
America, but the Brooklyn
Atlantics made the claim anyway.

CHAMPIONS OF AMERICA.

c. 1860s Before the color line
(*left*) While not exactly welcomed with open arms, black players did take part in baseball in the early days, including forming all-black teams.

c. 1860s School ball
As the game spread, college athletes began to form baseball teams in the 1860s and 1870s, including this unidentified team (*above*).

c. 1868 Our turn

Forward-thinking female students were among the first women to take up the game. This team from Vassar played regularly as a club until their mothers complained and the club was disbanded.

1869 The first pros

A day at the ballpark turned into payday (officially) for the first time with the formation of the Cincinnati Red Stockings in 1869 (*above*). Led by brothers Harry and George Wright, the team was the first to make baseball a professional sport. They played well, too, finishing their first season 65-0. This team photo was taken by famed Civil War photographer Matthew Brady.

1871 Baseball's champion

Few people have had as much impact on baseball—and with helping baseball make an impact on the world—as Albert Goodwill Spalding. First an ace pitcher in the fledgling pro American Association (he led his league in wins for six seasons), and later a promoter and sporting goods manufacturer, Spalding helped put baseball firmly into America's consciousness.

1874 How to do it

Early star George Wright (*right*) demonstrates all the techniques a 19th-century ballplayer might use. Notice that he does it all without the use of any gloves.

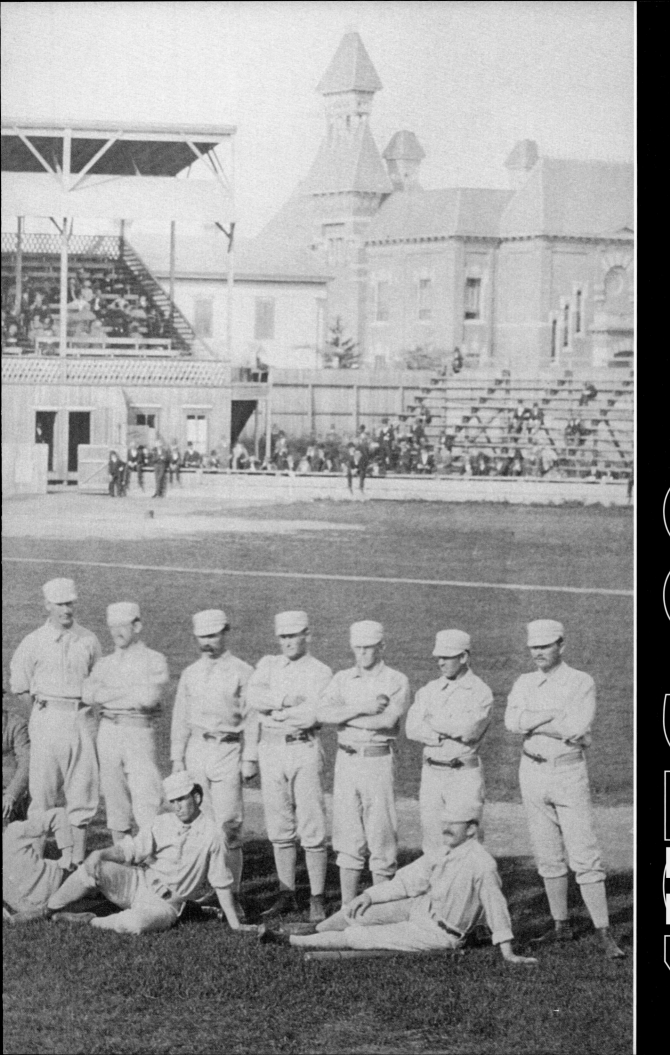

1876-99

1876-99
The Game Grows

It's difficult to say that many good things came out of the devastation of the Civil War. Obviously, the country stayed together and slavery ended . . . that's not bad. Another positive result was the spread of baseball by soldiers.

By the end of the war and into the 1870s, baseball was already being referred to in print as "the national game." As more and more people both learned to play and clamored to watch top players, the professionals began to take a firmer grasp on the game.

In February, 1876, out of the remains of two other leagues, the National League was formed by eight teams in a Manhattan hotel suite. Most historians use this date to mark the birth of the Major Leagues.

More than ever before, a regular annual schedule was kept; uniform rules were enforced; and conduct among league teams was more regulated, especially when that conduct dealt with player movement. However, the relationship between players and owners would never be a sweet one, and it is the same today as it was back then.

Notwithstanding the occasional reports that hearkened back to the game's "pure" origins, pro baseball flourished. New heroes were born, such as "King" Kelly, Cap Anson, Pud Galvin, and others.

Baseball became a part of the culture, as players began to appear on baseball cards, which were originally packaged with cigarettes and tobacco. The first "national championships" were held between and within leagues.

One of the most enduring legacies of this period was the poem "Casey at the Bat," written in 1888 by Ernest L. Thayer.

In the poem, the powerful Casey has the crowd on its feet, enthralled, as he tries to win the big game.

The poem ends, as all fans know, with the immortal words, ". . .mighty Casey has struck out." But while Casey whiffed, baseball was poised to hit a homer in the new century.

1876 The new league
Chicago White Stockings owner
William Hulbert spearheaded creation
of the National League this year, starting with eight teams.

c. 1880s Early slugger
"Big Dan" Brouthers was one of baseball's first big hitters, leading the N.L. in both batting average and home runs several times. A first baseman, he had the highest slugging percentage of any player in the 19th century.

1884 An early Robinson
Just a few years before baseball's owners agreed not to hire black players, Moses Fleetwood Walker (*left*) played for the Toledo franchise in the American Association. He and a few others would be the last black players in the majors for more than 50 years.

1885 Baseball Cap
Adrian "Cap" Anson was the most talented player of the century, batting better than .300 in 24 seasons. He also was Chicago's manager for a time.

c. 1880s Mr. Everything
John Montgomery Ward (*above*) could do it all . . . literally. He excelled as a pitcher, once throwing a perfect game, was a top shortstop and fine hitter, and helped organize the Brotherhood. He also managed a championship team and earned a law degree.

1887 Before Babe
The 137 home runs of gloveless first baseman Roger Connor was the all-time career best until Babe Ruth reached that total in 1921.

Copyright by
Goodwin & Co. N.Y.
1887.

1888 A signal achievement
Why do umpires make "safe" and "out" signals with their hands? Because of this man, William Hoy, the first pro player who was deaf. He was unable to hear the shouted signals of the time, so umps developed the hand signals still used today.

1890 Slide, Kelly, slide!
Before the Babe, before Joe DiMaggio, before Michael Jordan, America had a national sports hero–dashing, talented Michael "King" Kelly, a skilled player with matinee-idol looks.

1876-99

1890 The Players' League
Baseball's first player revolt came this
season as the fledgling Brotherhood of
Professional Base Ball Players formed
their own league. More than 60 major
leaguers defected, but the league lasted
only one year. Cleveland's entry, the
Spiders (*right*), finished near the bottom.

1890 Ladies days
Playing in long skirts in front of
crowds more curious about their
gender than their skills, teams such
as this one (*following pages*)
barnstormed around the country.

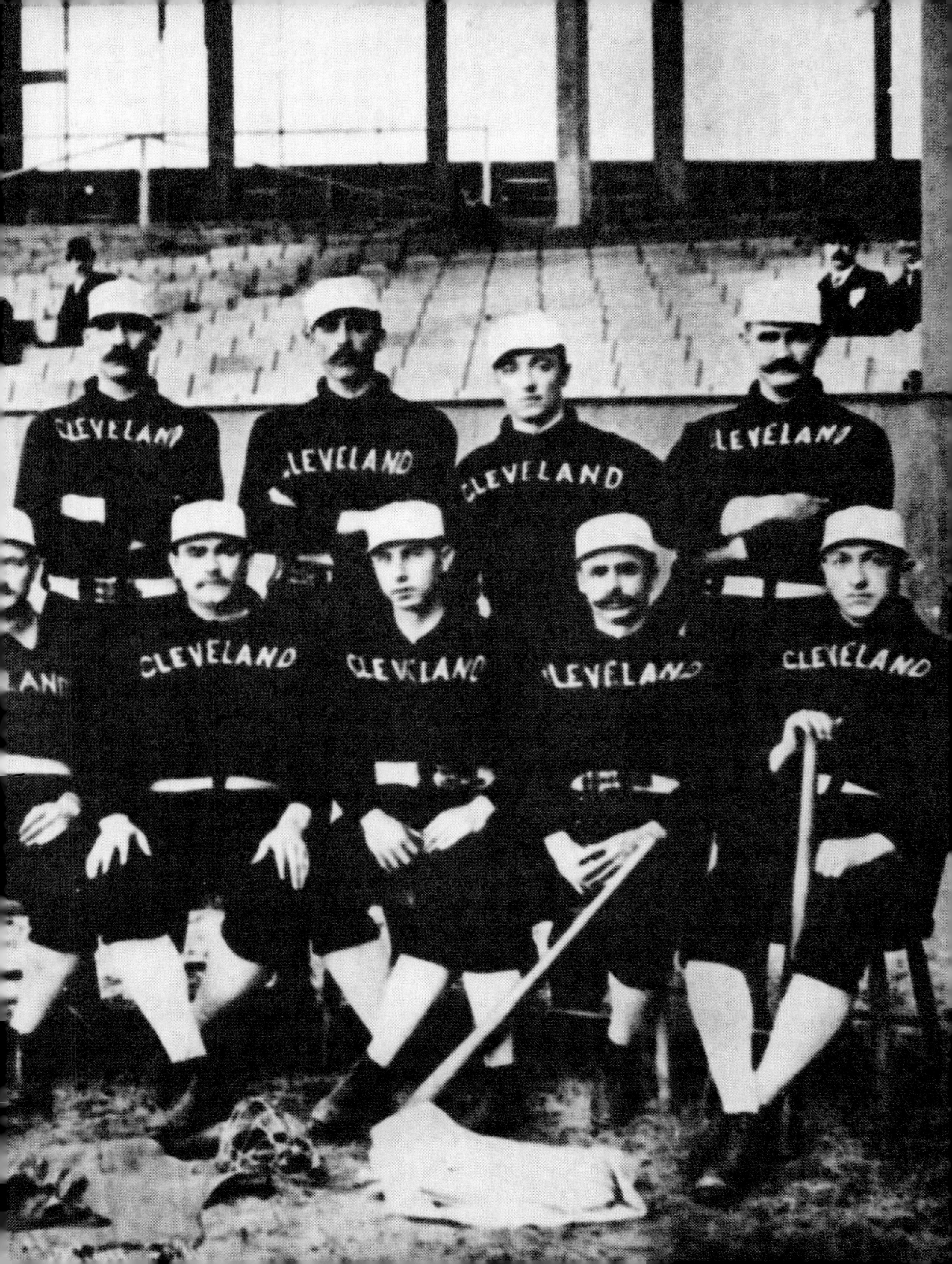
CLEVELAND

c. 1890 The Hoosier Thunderbolt
How hard did Indiana native Amos Rusie (*left*) throw the ball? Hard enough to change the rules of the game. After he struck out more than 900 batters from 1890 to 1892, the pitching mound was moved back five feet.

1897 Hit 'em where they ain't
That slogan, and a keen batting eye, made "Wee" Willie Keeler (*above*) famous. His 44-game hitting streak in 1897 remains tied for best ever in the National League; that season, he had an astounding .424 batting average.

1897 Secret superstar
Jake Beckley (*above*), second all-time in games played at first base and fourth all-time in triples, bridged the gap between centuries, playing until 1907.

1898 Remember the *Maine*
The original caption on this photo (*right*) of the USS *Maine*'s baseball team was "All blown up but one." J. H. Bloomer (top left) survived the devastating blast in Havana Harbor that touched off the Spanish-American War.

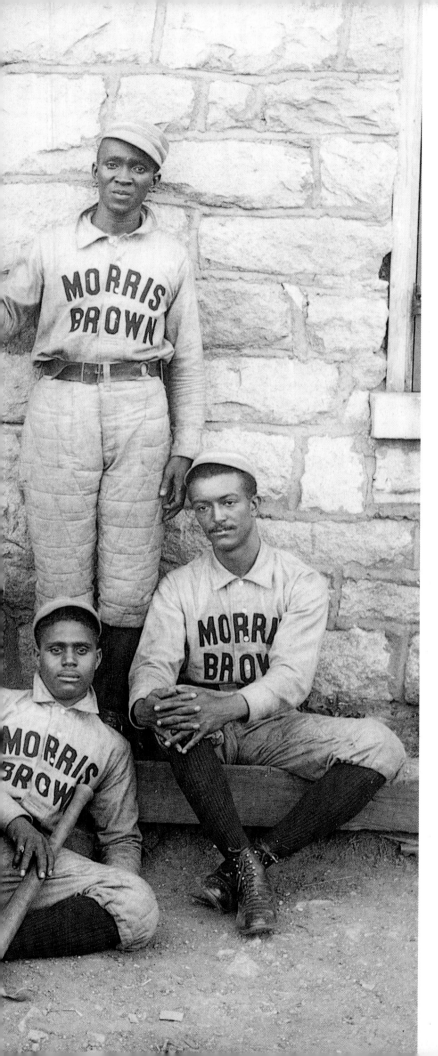

1899 The old college try
Though not allowed to play for
pay, these players could play for
school pride, representing Morris
Brown College in Atlanta.

1900s

Welcome the World Series
1900s

1903 Crowding the plate
The crowd spills onto the field at Boston's Huntington Grounds (*previous pages*) at the end of Game 1 of the first World Series, later won by Boston in eight games.

1903 Cheap seats
The craze for baseball is evident as these fans (*left*) go to any heights–literally–for a peek at one of the World Series games.

1901 First of many
The bowler-hatted man at the center (*above*) is Cornelius McGillicuddy, known to one and all as Connie Mack. This 1901 team was the first of 50 Athletics teams he would manage, and also later own, in baseball's longest career on the bench.

The new century in baseball began with the acceptance of a new "major" league. In 1901, the American League, built from the teams of the American Association, officially (and after much rancor) gained equal footing with the National League. Though briefly challenged on a couple of occasions, this two-league format has remained pro baseball's basic top-level structure.

The pairing was acrimonious at first, but cooler heads (shown the error of interleague fighting in the past) decided that cooperation meant success for everyone. They remained separate entities, but were joined now in a common pursuit of success and popularity.

Now that they were a pair, it seemed that a postseason championship should determine which league's top team was the greater. Thus in 1903, the World Series was born. In that first Series, the A.L.'s Boston Pilgrims defeated the N.L.'s Pittsburgh Pirates five games to three in the best-of-nine series. (It would later switch, with a couple of exceptions, to a best-of-seven event.)

The national craze for the World Series among fans and nonfans alike pointed to the game's continuing climb to the top of the sports pyramid. It had quickly surpassed other pursuits and, while it would later be challenged by other pro sports, baseball used the World Series as a springboard to national prominence.

Aiding baseball's rise in this decade were notable stars, among them pitcher Christy Mathewson of the Giants, as noble a person as he was outstanding as a pitcher. In the 1905 Series, he threw three shutouts, a record that still stands.

Cy Young was also winning dozens of ball games, while Ty Cobb and Honus Wagner were just beginning their remarkable careers.

Away from the spotlight, Negro leagues were forming for black players excluded from the major leagues.

1900s

1904 View from the bleachers
The Chicago White Stockings host the Boston Red Sox in this 1904 game (*above*). Notice the fans on the field crowding the left field foul line.

1904 "Iron Man"
A boyhood job in an Illinois foundry gave Joe McGinnity his nickname. He made it stand up in the majors, setting a two-year record for innings pitched (842 in 1903-04) and pitching five doubleheaders, including three in one month.

1905 End of an era
Big Ed Delahanty (*right*) wrapped up an amazing career with Washington in 1905. His career average of .346 is fourth-best all-time. Supposedly, he once hit a ball so hard, he broke it in half.

1905 Young Georgia Peach
This fresh-faced young man (*left*) began one of baseball's most remarkable careers in 1905. Tyrus Raymond Cobb was just 19 years old when he made his debut with the Detroit Tigers. Two years later, he began a never-matched string of 12 consecutive N.L. batting titles.

1905 Super shortstop
The tendency in the days of racially separated baseball was to compare one set of players to the other. Thus the outstanding play at shortstop of John "Pop" Lloyd (*right*) earned him the nickname "The Black Honus Wagner." So adept at fielding was Lloyd that the great Wagner considered the reference an honor.

1900s Down on the farms
Not every player could make the Majors . . . or even the minors. Semipro teams like this anonymous one (*below*) played throughout the East and Midwest, facing off against each other or against lower-level pro teams and town teams.

1905 What a Rube
It's hard to say whether being a bit crazy made Rube
Waddell a better pitcher, or whether his lightning
arm succeeded in spite of his goofy brain. In 1904,
Waddell, baseball's original "character," set a record
for strikeouts (349) that stood until 1973.

c. 1900s "Cy" for Cyclone

Baseball's most unbreakable record? Here's a vote for the career victory total of 511, a mark set by Denton True "Cy" Young (*above*). Baseball's best pitchers today earn an annual award named for the longtime Indians and Red Sox hurler.

1907 Away from the spotlight

Not every champion played in the World Series. Each of the dozens of minor leagues crowned champions, who were every bit as proud as their Major League counterparts of their pennants. Here (*following pages*) is the Burlington team that captured the rather enormous Iowa State League flag.

1900s

Early 1900s Going co-ed
Several teams of "Bloomer Girls" donned the clothing of the same name to create traveling exhibition teams (*above*). While the main draw was the female players, many male players also participated. Future Major League stars such as "Smoky" Joe Wood and Rogers Hornsby played on Bloomer Girls teams.

1907 Opposite of ignorant
Catchers' gear, later famously dubbed the "tools of ignorance," was rudimentary in the early days. Roger Bresnahan refined it and introduced the first leather shin guards this season (*right*).

1908 End of the stanza
Along with fame earned poetically, Frank
Chance was a top-flight manager, leading
the Cubs to four N.L. pennants in five
years, adding a World Series title in 1908.
It would be the hapless Cubbies' final title
of the century.

1908 Start of a Poem
"These are the saddest of possible words/Tinker to Evers to Chance . . ." So goes baseball's second most famous poem. Because of it, an otherwise somewhat pedestrian double play combination of Joe Tinker (*above*), Johnny Evers, and Frank Chance (*opposite*) became baseball legends.

1908 Atop Coogan's Bluff
High above the Polo Grounds (*following pages*), Giants fans filled the hills to watch the dramatic finish to the 1908 National League season. The game on the field is a replay of the famous "Merkle's Boner" game. That game was declared a tie on September 23 after a disputed baserunning mistake. The two teams finished with identical records, necessitating a replay. But Chicago won, 4-2, defeating the Giants ace pitcher Christy Mathewson.

1908 Famous for forgetting
For forgetting to touch second base as a winning run scored, Giants outfielder Fred Merkle (*left*) cost his team a victory, and later, many said, a pennant. "Merkle's Boner" is one of baseball's legendary goofs.

1908 Only the good die young
Another sad baseball case is that of pitcher Addie Joss (*above*). In a nine-year career cut short by his death at 31 from meningitis, he fashioned the second-best ERA ever at 1.89, and pitched a perfect game in 1908.

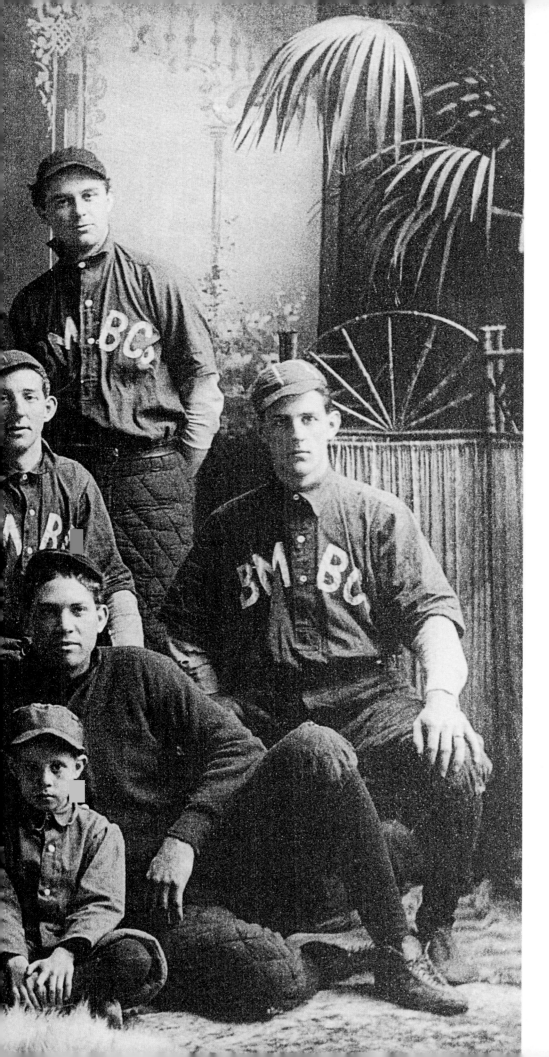

1909 Northern champs
Though not yet a state, Alaska nonetheless took heartily to America's game. This team from Juneau was the Alaska League champion in 1909.

1909 Caught in the action
Photographs this well-lit and with this
much action were rare in baseball's
early days; this shot from New York's
Hilltop Park is especially good.

1909 The other Babe
Pittsburgh rookie Babe Adams (*right*)
got his career off to a flying start in
the World Series, with three victories
over Ty Cobb's Detroit Tigers in the
Pirates' title run.

1909 Philly's ace
Albert Bender earned his then-politically-correct nickname of "Chief" because he was half Chippewa Indian. He was all pitcher, too, helping the Athletics win three World Series titles.

1909 Crisp action
Neither Washington's Otis Clymer, batting, nor New York's Red Kleinow, catching, had remarkable careers. Yet they held their poses well for this classic baseball tableau.

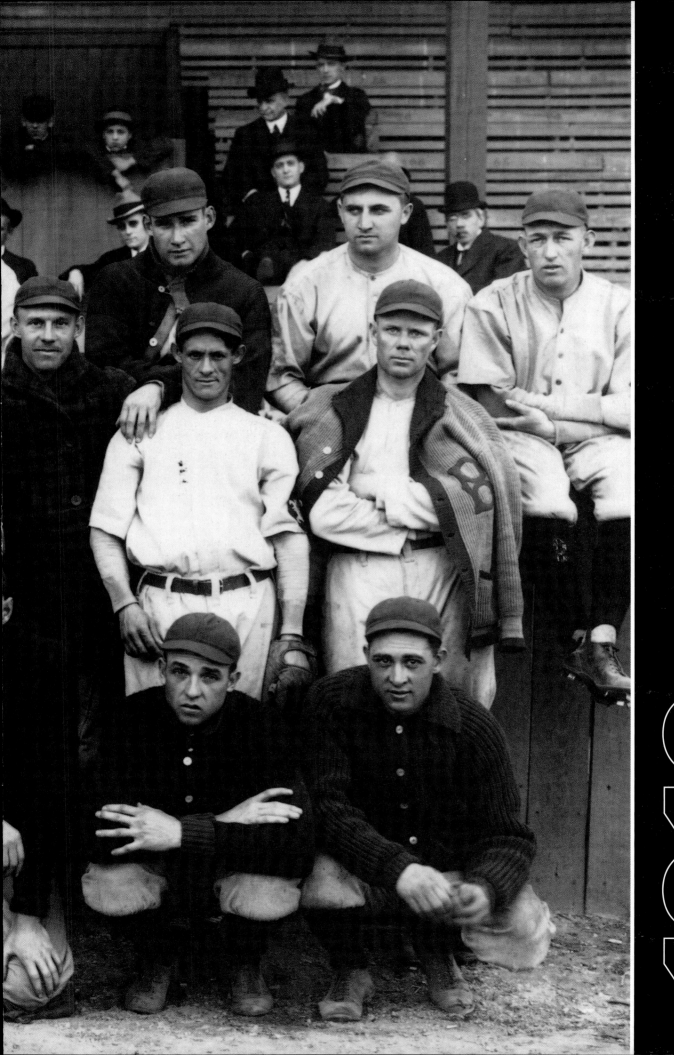

1910s
High Hopes and Black Sox

1912 Our game
The continuing rise of the Major Leagues floated all boats. This group of players (*previous pages*) in Richmond, Virginia, prepares to open the 1912 minor-league season in that town.

1910 Big pitch
A tradition was born in 1910, when President William Howard Taft (*above*) attended the opening game of the Washington Senators' and threw out the ceremonial first pitch. It's been an annual presidential rite ever since.

1916 War and Remembrance
Legendary pitcher Christy Mathewson ended his career in 1916, so he could serve in World War I. Perhaps the finest pitcher of his generation, Mathewson suffered poison gas burns in European fighting and died young in 1925.

With the Major Leagues a decade old, baseball had become, truly, the National Pastime, intensely followed by devoted millions, the sport of choice for boys from Maine to Missouri. The World Series became a spectacle that transfixed the populace, even in these days before radio.

In this decade, the business of baseball blossomed, as teams, realizing the value and importance of new and glamorous ballparks (presaging another renovation boom that revamped the face of baseball in the last decade of the 20th century), built some of the most famous baseball parks. Ebbets Field, the Polo Grounds, Tiger Stadium, and Fenway Park all saw their first games in the first half of this decade, but only Fenway survived to see a new century.

Though the spectacle of hitting, running, and pitching was the key draw, the unifying force of the game was perhaps its greatest attraction. At the turn of the century, America was a blooming nation of immigrants seeking identity yet again as a remade polyglot of peoples. In baseball these different groups found a common language.

Then, suddenly, it seemed, the honeymoon was over. The communal love of the game faced two stern tests as this decade drew to a close. The first was World War I, but the game played on throughout the war; it survived that test relatively unscathed.

The second test came in 1919 with the "Black Sox Scandal," in which a group of Chicago White Sox players conspired with gamblers to throw the World Series. The facts of the scandal are still controversial today, but this stain on the national game nearly buried it. The innocence of the sport was lost and its ties to the world of commerce forever bared.

Fortunately for baseball, there was a force growing in this decade that would serve to lift baseball higher than it had ever been . . . a force called Babe.

1910 The way West
On their way to spring training in San Francisco, the Chicago White Sox (*left*) pose for a train-side picture. Even then, owners were taking the game to lucrative new markets.

1910 It worked for him
Detroit star Ty Cobb (*above*) shows off the unorthodox batting style–note the separated hands–that helped him dominate the game for nearly two decades.

c. 1910s The other champs
The Lincoln Giants, New York's
"other" Giants, were one of the
Negro League's dominant teams
in this decade, winning a key battle
with the Chicago Americans to
claim a "national" title.

1910s

1912 Building champions
Across America, leagues of all sorts were springing up. As this Burlington, Iowa, team (*above*) proudly shows, a champion's a champion, no matter how small.

c. 1910s Champion builder
A former player and manager, the legendarily pecunious Charles Comiskey (*right*) helped found the American League and owned the White Sox for more than 30 years.

1910s

1912 Early cyber-baseball
At the 1912 World Series, the national need for news led to this section of telegraphers at New York's Polo Grounds, keymasters who rapidly sent word of the games to the world.

1910s

1912 Over too soon
Before he was 25 years old, Boston Red
Sox pitcher "Smokey" Joe Wood had won
101 games, including 34 this season. He
ended his career in 1920 with only 117.

1913 Baseball Olympian
As much gate attraction as player, double gold medalist Jim Thorpe turned from track and field to bat and glove, joining the Giants for the first of his six undistinguished Major League seasons. He went on to help found the NFL.

1913 Pregame pitching
Loosening up before a game in Cincinnati
(*top*) are a quartet of Reds, including
"Three Fingers" Brown at far right and at
the tail end of a Hall of Fame career.

1913 The only one
There have been some awesome sluggers in baseball
history, but only one was called "Home Run." Frank
"Home Run" Baker earned his famous nickname by
clouting a league-leading 12 homers in 1913.

1913 The Giants are giants
A capacity crowd packs the Polo Grounds to cheer on the New York Giants (*above*). Their support wasn't enough to help the Giants win the series, as the mighty Philadelphia Athletics won the title in five games, led by pitcher "Chief" Bender.

1914 Another league leaves a legacy
(*following pages*) The Whales, the Chicago entry in the short-lived Federal League, left behind one of baseball's gems: Wrigley Field, much-beloved, ivy-covered home to the Chicago Cubs since the Whales' folding.

1914 The Miracle Braves

In last place and trailing by 14 games in mid-July, the Boston Braves stormed back to win the N.L. pennant. In the World Series, catcher Hank Gowdy (*left*) hit .545 and the Braves swept the Athletics.

1915 Pre-Babe

While Babe Ruth was still a pitcher, Gavvy Cravath of the Phillies (*above*) was setting the home run pace. He led the N.L. with 24 this season, setting the bar for Ruth.

1915 The Dutchman

Win a trivia contest by knowing this: Honus Wagner (*previous pages*) got more votes for the Hall of Fame than Babe Ruth. The peerless shortstop, a career .324 hitter, batted better than .300 for 17 consecutive seasons, stole 722 bases, and earned respect from teammates and opponents alike for his great character and generosity.

1915 Baseball's Napoleon

Napoleon Lajoie, shown here with the Athletics at the end of his career, was such a huge star in Cleveland that for a time, the team was renamed the "Naps." A .338 lifetime hitter, Lajoie was also one of the best-fielding second basemen ever.

1916 Early greatness
This could be any bunch of local-champion city kids with slick uniforms were it not for the presence of the young slugger at the bottom right, a kid named Lou Gehrig.

1916 Caught in the act
Brooklyn Robins catcher Chief Myers (*above*) slashes the ball and heads toward first in this great example of early baseball action photography. Myers and the Robins lost to Boston, however, in five games.

1916 Field generals
Brooklyn manager Wilbert Robinson (*left*) greets Boston manager Bill Corrigan before the World Series, won by Boston in five games with help from a kid named Ruth.

1918 Hippo gets hot
A solid pitcher, James "Hippo" Vaughn (*right*) had his best season in 1918, leading the league with 23 wins, 148 strikeouts, and a 1.74 ERA and helping the Cubs win a rare N.L. pennant.

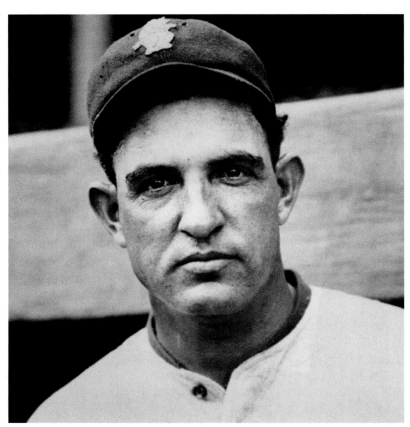

1918 War ball
Baseball went to war along with the world at the end of the decade. These Canadian soldiers (*left*) turned to the game to help recuperate from battlefield wounds.

1918 Baseball's King
The bearded gent (*below*) is King George V of England. American soldiers in his country during World War I brought their game with them, and he stopped by to meet some players.

1918 The complete player
Though Babe Ruth (*right*) would soon rewrite the record books as a slugger, and capture the world's attention as an icon, he began his career as an ace lefty for the Boston Red Sox, helping them win three pennants.

1918 Brooklyn's best boy

In a borough that made its baseball heroes part of the family, few Brooklyn Dodgers were more beloved than outfielder Zach Wheat. He played for the "Trolley-Dodgers" (the origin of the team's nickname) for 18 years, racking up a career .317 average.

1919 Say it ain't so

The case of Joe Jackson (*right*), owner of the third-best career batting average, is one of the saddest to come out of the 1919 Black Sox scandal. Though Jackson allegedly took money, some argue that he didn't really understand his actions. He hit .375 with six RBI in the Series, and to all acounts played his hardest. Yet for his role in the affair, he remains banned from his otherwise deserved place in the Hall of Fame.

1919 The Black Sox

They were supposed to be the champions. They were supposed to be the best team in baseball. Instead, the 1919 Chicago White Sox went down in baseball infamy, as eight players took part in a bribery conspiracy to throw the World Series to the Reds.

YANKEE STADIUM

1920S

1920s
The Golden Age

1923 Palace for a golden age
(*previous pages*) Yankee Stadium opened on April 18, 1923. In the first game played there, Babe Ruth hit a home run . . . of course. The park became known as "The House That Ruth Built."

c. 1920s Titanic Twosome
Though of vastly different temperaments, the serious Lou Gehrig and the bombastic Babe Ruth (*left*) possessed nearly equal levels of skills never before seen in baseball. Their astounding hitting feats, many of which are still unmatched, helped the Yankees win 5 World Series in this decade.

1921 A singularly triple feat
Bill Wambsganss (*above*, far left) poses with three men who "helped" him make history. In the 1920 World Series, Cleveland second baseman "Wamby" caught Clarence Mitchell's liner, doubled off Pete Kilduff, and tagged Otto Miller to complete the only unassisted triple play in Series history and one of fewer than a dozen ever in baseball.

The 1920s have been called the "Golden Age of Sports." During the decade, some of the most resonant and important figures in a wide variety of sports were at the top of their games.

In golf, Bobby Jones set standards which are only now being met. In boxing, Jack Dempsey was creating his own legend. Red Grange, the Galloping Ghost, helped make pro football popular. And in tennis, Bill Tilden was a dominant figure.

But in baseball, one player emerged who not only dwarfed all those others, but towered over baseball and America as no athlete has before or since. He was George Herman Ruth.

The Babe.

Babe Ruth was already well-known to baseball fans for his pitching prowess with the Boston Red Sox. But when his contract was sold to the New York Yankees before the 1920 season (an event that sparked Boston's "Curse of the Bambino" legend), Ruth moved from the mound to rightfield. His powerful bat was soon clouting home runs so numerous and massive that a new adjective was born–"Ruthian"–still used today to describe over-sized feats on the diamond.

In 1920, his first season in Yankee pinstripes, he hit 54 home runs, nearly doubling a record he had set only a year earlier. The total was more than all but one team

hit that season. His 1920 slugging average of .847 is still an all-time record.

By the end of the 1921 season, he had become baseball's all-time leading home run hitter; he would not be removed from that spot until the 1974 season, by Hank Aaron.

Ruth's outlandish personality was as big as his bat, and he soon outdistanced baseball itself to become a national celebrity. He helped the Yankees win six A.L. pennants and three World Series in the decade. And in 1927, he hit 60 home runs. Though that mark has since been topped several times, no one can ever top the Babe and his lasting impact on baseball, sports, and America.

1920s

1920 The baby Babe
To this day, Boston Red Sox fans rue
the day that Boston owner Harry
Frazee sold star Babe Ruth (*above*)
to the Yankees to finance a new
Broadway play. In his first season with
New York, Ruth slugged 54 home runs,
the first of his four 50-homer seasons.

1920 Here comes the Judge
Stung by the Black Sox Scandal,
baseball's owners turned to the
crusty Judge Kenesaw Mountain
Landis (*right*) to serve in the
all-powerful new position of
Commissioner. He ruled the game
with an iron hand until 1944.

1920s

1921 Still a star
While the new "lively" ball and the home run swing took over baseball in the decade, Ty Cobb (*previous pages*) continued his unyielding style of play. He adapted his game nicely, thank you, batting .334 and above each year from 1920 to 1927, including .401 in 1922.

1921 Giants of baseball
Though the Yankees dominated baseball for most of the decade, they lost the first two World Series to their crosstown rival, the New York Giants (*above*). Here, Ross Youngs of the Giants scores in Game 3 of his team's 1921 championship series victory.

132

1922 Modern methods
Teams had been traveling south and west for warmer spring (though technically late winter) weather since baseball's early days. Here, Brooklyn Dodgers players warm up in the protective batting cage. In later years, machines replaced pitchers in these cages.

1923 The Sultan of Swat
Volumes could be written—and have been—about Ruth's monumental achievements as a hitter. "I swing big and I miss big," he said, as he proved here in this rarely-seen 1923 photograph. He remains the single most important player in baseball history.

1924 Way out West
Though Major League teams would not call the West Coast home for 30 more years, the Pacific Coast League was a flourishing minor league. (*above*) Members of the Sacramento team are greeted with flowers at the season opening game.

1924 Some valuable ducats
In a photograph that shows both the relative innocence and importance of the game in that age (*right*), Washington D.C. policemen guard this shipment of World Series tickets as it arrives at the ballpark, hand-carried by club employees.

1920s

1924 That's not cricket!
No, it's baseball, and the New York Giants and Chicago Cubs showed King George V how the game was played during an offseason tour of Great Britain. Though played sporadically in its ancestral home, baseball has not spread to the United Kingdom as it has to other nations.

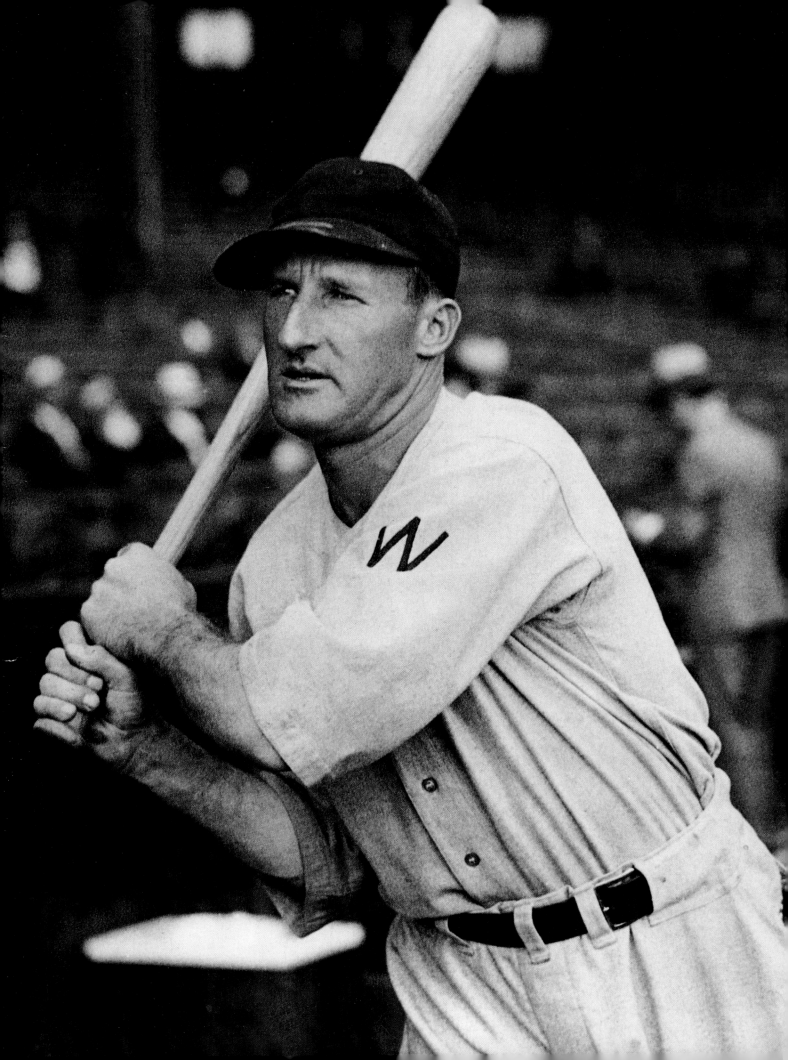

1924 Take a gander at Goose
Though overshadowed by stars in other cities, Goose Goslin (*left*) was one of the American League's top hitters in the 1920s. In 1924, he led the league with 129 RBI while helping the Washington Senators win their first and only World Series championship.

1924 But for a pebble . . .
Hard-luck Giants third baseman Fred Lindstrom (*above*) is baseball's epitome of the bad bounce. In the 1924 World Series, ground balls hit pebbles or rocks and bounced over his head twice, the second time bringing in the Series-clinching run for Washington. Lindstrom recovered to put together a Hall of Fame career.

1920s

1924 Way "over there"
American servicemen were taking the game around the world, helping start leagues in Japan, among other places. These Marines pose with a championship banner from their posting on the Pacific island of Guam. A championship's a championship, no matter where won.

143

1920s

1924 Pre-game pose
Though the Senators (team on left, *above*) were saddled with one of the most depressing team "slogans" in history–"Washington: First in war, first in peace, and last in the American League"–they finally were champions. They defeated the Giants after posing for this shot before the Series-deciding seventh game.

1924 The Rajah
Perhaps the greatest righthanded hitter in history, Cardinals second baseman Rogers Hornsby (*right*) dominated the National League in the 1920s. He won seven batting titles in the decade, including one in 1924 with a mark of .424, the best single-season average in the 20th century. He ended his splendid career at the plate with a stunning .358 batting average, good for second best all-time.

1924 The Fordham Flash
Frankie Frisch (*left*) turned from college star to pro star almost overnight. A top-fielding second baseman and a fine hitter (13 seasons over .300), and later a manager, he was a winner wherever he played. As a player with the Giants and Cardinals from 1919 to 1937, he played on eight pennant winners, while finishing second in six other seasons.

1924 Big Chief and Big Train
(*following pages*) Washington Senators pitcher Walter "The Big Train" Johnson shows President Calvin Coolidge how he throws the fastball that earned him his nickname. Though presidents brought hometown biases to their new jobs, they often "adopted" the Senators, their new hometown team.

1920s

1924 Safe, but soon out
Yankees first baseman Wally Pipp (*above*) beat the tag on this play, but the next spring was not so lucky. Down with a cold, he watched young Lou Gehrig step in to take his place, a position Gehrig would not give up for more than 14 seasons.

c. 1920s Hey, Blue
Few umpires have achieved the status of legend. Bill Klem (*left*) was the first. An umpire from 1905 to 1940, he helped invent hand signals and worked a record 18 World Series. "I never missed a call," was how he summed up his Hall of Fame career.

c. 1920s "He was the best"
Many outstanding players took the field in the 1920s. Among the best, and among the best ever, was outfielder Oscar Charleston (*right*). An outstanding fielder with great speed, he was among Negro League leaders in batting average for many years, including a spectacular .434 season in 1921. No less a baseball judge than John McGraw called Charleston "the best . . . period."

c. 1920s Finally a champion

Washington's Walter Johnson (*left*) was perhaps the finest righthanded pitcher ever. His statistics are almost mindboggling. In an age when strikeouts were rare, he notched more than 3,500. He won 417 games, second-most all-time. He threw an all-time record 110 shutouts. He was durable: In 1913, he was 36-7 with a 1.14 ERA. Nearly a decade later, he helped the Senators win their only title by finishing 23-7 and was named MVP.

1924 Series action

Action photography from the 1920s is rare, but this shot (*above*) of a pitch from the 1924 World Series shows how very little the game has changed since then. Save for the photographers crowding home plate and the plethora of hats in the stands, this could have been taken last year.

1920s

1924 Caught in the act
Washington's Bucky Harris (*above*) is in
a pickle here, chased down between
the bases. The scrappy second baseman was a Senator for 10 seasons,
followed by a short stint with Detroit,
before a long career as a manager.

1924 Right man for the job
While Ruth, Gehrig, & Co. were
posting gaudy numbers on offense,
someone had to pitch for their string
of championship teams. From 1923
to 1928, Herb Pennock (*right*) had
an ERA greater than 3.00 only once,
and had a pair of 20-win seasons.

1926 to 1929 Bucketfoot Al

Few believed that the young slugger who "stepped in the bucket" would amount to much. All of them were wrong. Odd-swinging Al Simmons (*left*) had 11 seasons of 100 RBI or more and eight seasons of .340 or better. He helped the Athletics win N.L. pennants from 1929 to 1931.

c. 1920s Cool Papa Bell

Beneath the radar of most baseball fans, the Negro Leagues continued to provide a way for top black athletes to compete. One such was James "Cool Papa" Bell (*above*). Of Bell's legendary speed, Satchel Paige once said, "Cool Papa's so fast, he can turn off the light and be in bed before the room gets dark."

1920s

1926 Played in the minds' eye
Fans at this Los Angeles-area telegraph station (*above*) cluster around a diamond chalked on a blackboard. As pitch-by-pitch results from the 1926 World Series arrive via telegraph, they are put on the board and announced with a megaphone. Similar scenes could be found from coast to coast.

1926 Welcome home, Cards
After defeating the mighty New York Yankees in seven thrilling games to win the World Series, the St. Louis Cardinals were welcomed home with an enormous, street-filling parade.

1926 Dive, Mickey!
Gordon "Mickey" Cochrane has to be included in any discussion of the greatest catchers of all time. Not only was he a top hitter, but, as this dramatic action photograph (*following pages*) shows, he went all-out defensively as well.

1926 The old man
Old and somewhat past his prime, Grover Cleveland "Pete" Alexander (*left*) nevertheless gave baseball one of its greatest moments. In the seventh inning of Game 7 of the 1926 World Series, he struck out Yankee slugger Tony Lazzeri with the bases loaded and then shut down New York for two more innings to give the Cardinals the world championship.

c. 1920s Brooklyn's hero
Wilbert Robinson (*above*), manager of the Brooklyn National League club, was so beloved by his team and his fans that for much of his time as manager, the team was renamed the Robins in his honor. A former top player, he led Brooklyn from 1914 to 1931.

1927 He tamed the Babe
Miller Huggins (*left*) managed the Yankees from 1918 until his sudden death in 1929. Under him, the team won six pennants and three World Series, and his 1927 squad is considered one of, if not the, best ever. But perhaps his greatest skill was in working with and nearly controlling the force that was Babe Ruth.

1927 60!

Babe Ruth accomplished many things on the baseball diamond, even as he was building a legend off it. But in 1927, he claimed forever a unique spot: The first player ever with 60 home runs in a single season. For the rest of the century, that mark would be a touchstone, twice sparking sports-world-shattering chases to topple it. And though the mark has now been topped, Ruth has never lost his own singular place at the summit.

c. 1920s The end of an era nears

With the big bang school of baseball now dominant, old-school manager John McGraw (*above*) saw his remarkable career coming to a close. The man known as "Little Napoleon" for his control of a game would eventually retire in 1933 as manager of the Giants, after having won 2,784 games, second-most ever, and leading New York to 10 N.L. pennants.

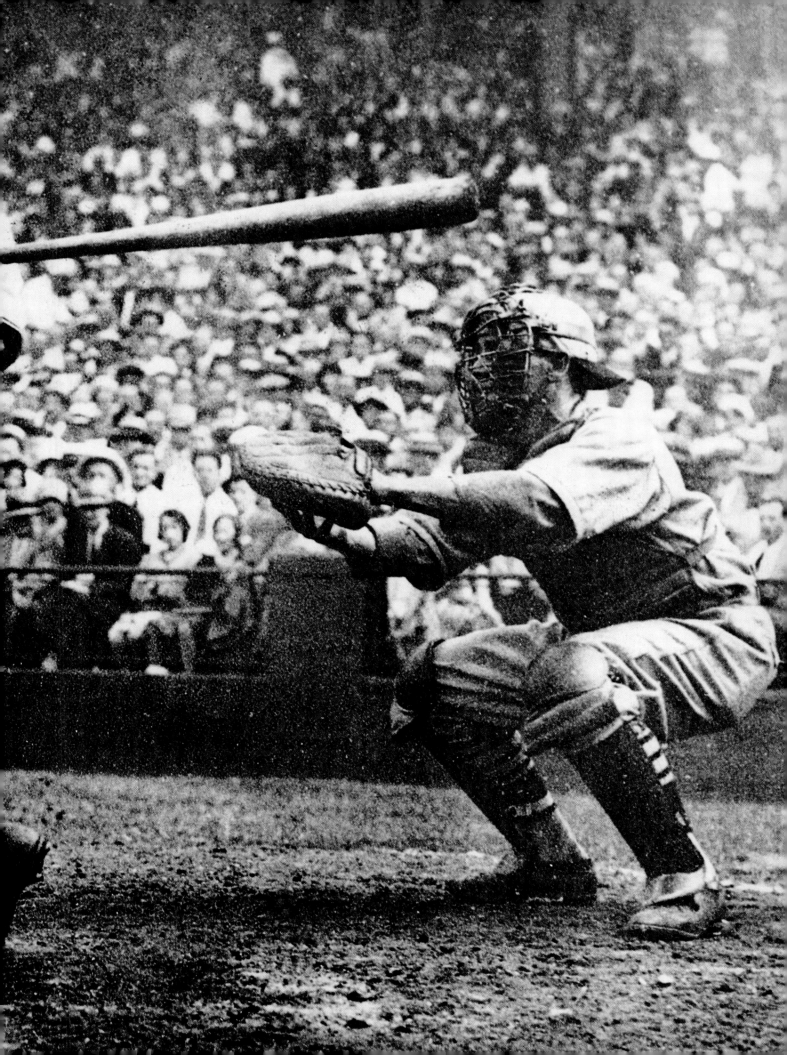

1920s

1929 Hack takes a hack
This evocative photo of slugger Hack Wilson (*previous pages*) is among the most famous of the period. The squat but powerful Cubs outfielder was stunning in 1929 (.356, 159 RBI) and 1930 (.345, a then N.L. record 56 homers, and an all-time record 190 RBI).

1929 Who needs a ticket?
Presaging Cubs fans outside Wrigley Field by 50 years or so, fans packed the rooftops behind the outfield walls of Philadelphia's Shibe Park for a glimpse of their Athletics' triumph in the 1929 World Series.

1930s
The Yankee Years

1933 Schoolboy ball
A sunny day, a baseball diamond, and boys at play: A perfect recipe for an iconic American scene, captured here at the Hotchkiss School in Connecticut (*previous pages*).

1935 I got it!
On the fabled Yankee teams of the 1930s, Bill Dickey (*left*) was a quiet star, overshadowed by more famous players. The great-hitting catcher was named to the Hall of Fame in 1954.

1936 Fabulous foursome
(*above*) Dickey is joined by Lou Gehrig, Joe DiMaggio, and Tony Lazzeri prior to the World Series, the second of five that the Yankees would win in the 1930s.

The overarching force in America in the 1930s was the Depression. In baseball, however, it was the Yankees.

Through the Roaring Twenties, baseball rebounded–thanks largely to Babe Ruth–from the Black Sox scandal. Now the game faced a new challenge with the Depression. Attendance shrank dramatically, teams were forced to sell top players for cash, and some minor league teams folded altogether. Fans were sometimes forced to decide whether they would eat or go to the ballpark.

But as it had before, baseball rallied through the troubles and produced some outstanding performances, by both individuals and teams.

No team was more outstanding than the New York Yankees. Led by a parade of stars that began with Ruth and Lou Gehrig and ended with Joe DiMaggio, New York won five World Series in the 1930s, including four in a row to end the decade, a streak since matched only by the Yankees of the 1950s.

Ruth was winding down and would retire by 1935, but still provided typical "Ruthian" moments, such as the 1932 World Series, when he supposedly "called his shot" by pointing to the centerfield bleachers before slugging a game-winning homer to those very seats.

Gehrig, too, saw the end of his fabled career, when he was struck down by amyotrophic lateral sclerosis (ALS), a disease that would come to bear his name.

Other great teams of the decade included the 1930 Philadelphia Athletics, the last of Hall of Fame manager Connie Mack's many great teams; and the 1934 St. Louis Cardinals, famed for their off-field antics and known as the "Gashouse Gang."

In 1936 the Baseball Hall of Fame was instituted. And baseball celebrated a false centennial in 1939, based on the now-disproven "Doubleday Myth."

Baseball, like America, survived the Depression. But a new challenge awaited the country and the game.

1931 That's my boy
Lou Gehrig was one of baseball's toughest competitors, but he was almost as famous for his devotion to his parents. Here he poses with his mother, Christina.

1931 Babe's babes
Babe Ruth had a well-deserved
reputation as something other than a
family man, a fact belied by this
pleasant scene with his adopted
daughters Dorothy and Julia.

1930s

1931 Female with a fastball
Seventeen-year-old Jackie Mitchell pitched briefly for a minor league team in the 1930s, one of only a handful of women ever to play pro ball. Though Gehrig and Ruth look on with amusement here, Mitchell allegedly struck out Ruth in an exhibition game.

c. 1930s The greatest ever?
Catcher Josh Gibson (*above*) may have slugged more than 800 home runs in his career. But since he was restricted to playing in the Negro Leagues, most fans never got to see the man some experts consider to be one of–if not *the*–greatest players of all time.

1932 Dazzlin' Dazzy
Brooklyn pitcher Dazzy Vance (*right*), as well known for his nightlife as his fastball, led the National League in strikeouts for a record seven consecutive seasons.

1930s

1933 The future
Future Yankees star Joe DiMaggio first found prominence as a teenager with his hometown San Francisco Seals of the Pacific Coast League.

1934 Land of the Rising Babe
In the twilight of his great career, Babe Ruth (*above*) was still an international icon. After the 1934 season, he led a group of stars on a goodwill trip to Japan.

1933 Go ahead, throw it
Detroit catcher Mickey Cochrane and Boston pitcher Lefty Grove model souvenir gloves given to them on their own tour of Japan.

1934 Red Sox rocket man
A star for Philadelphia and Boston, Grove (*right*) was perhaps the finest lefthanded pitcher ever.

1934 He's still got it
Proving that he didn't have to hit a home run to score, Babe Ruth (*following pages*) slides in safely in a game against Detroit.

1930s

1935 Other champions
Champions of the Negro Leagues this season, the Pittsburgh Crawfords (*following pages*) featured five future Hall of Fame players, including Oscar Charleston, first on the left.

1934 Marvelous Medwick
Cardinals outfielder Joe "Ducky" Medwick (*above*) led St. Louis to the 1934 World Series title and won the Triple Crown in 1937.

1934 Baseball's other Babe
Baseball was just one of the many sports at which Babe Didrickson (*right*), the century's greatest female athlete, excelled.

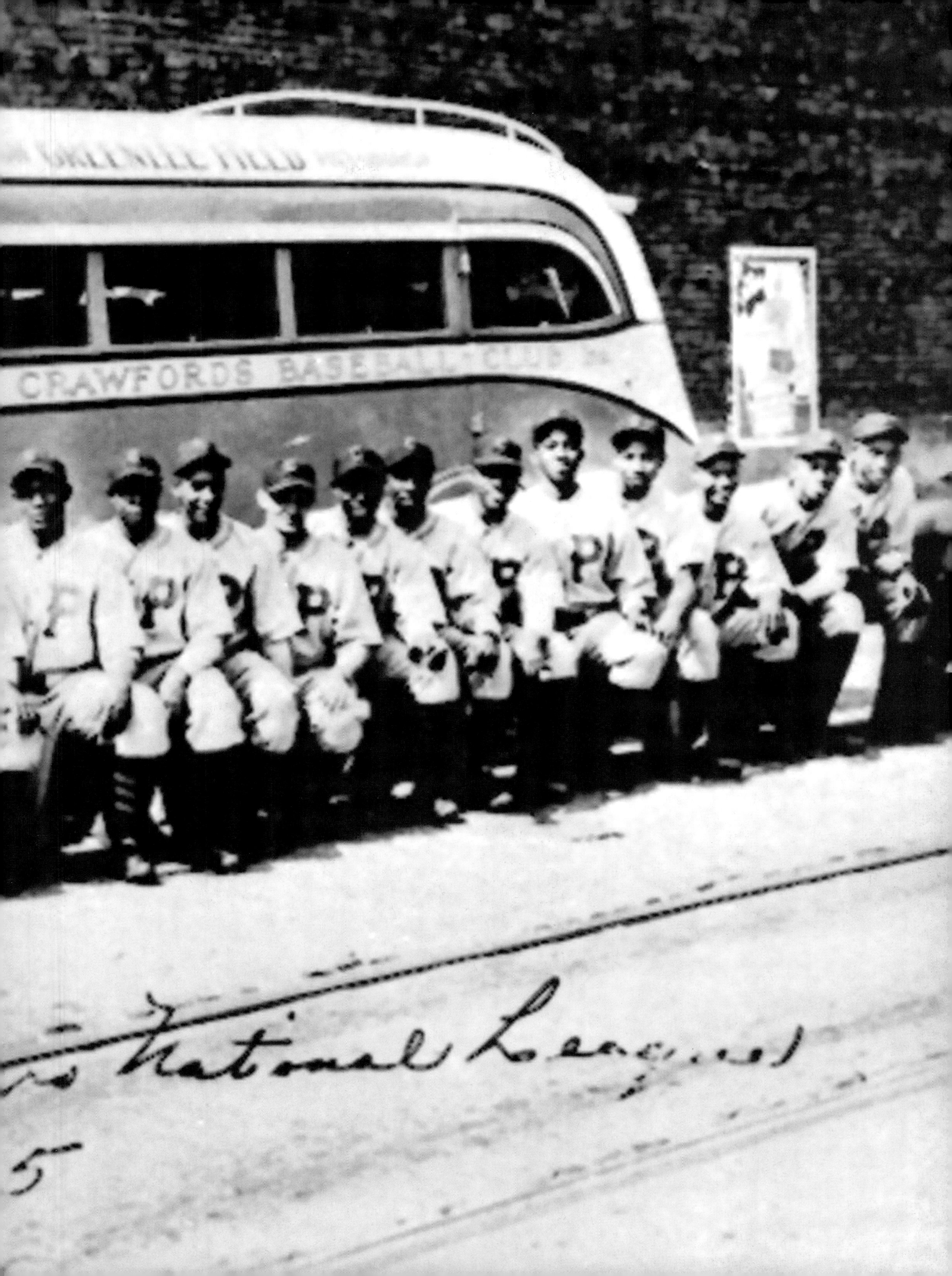
CRAWFORDS BASEBALL CLUB
National Leagues

1930s

1935 Let them shine
The first night games in Major League
Baseball history were played this
season in Crosley Field in Cincinnati
(*above*).

1935 Manager Mickey
One of baseball's all-time greatest
catchers, Detroit's Mickey Cochrane
(*right*) pulled double duty in 1935 by
also managing the Tigers.

1935 Pair of poisons
The hard-hitting Waner brothers (*left*),
Lloyd "Little Poison" and Paul "Big
Poison," played together in Pittsburgh
for 14 seasons.

1936 Stylin'
Facial hair was rare in baseball
in this era, but Brooklyn utility
man Frenchy Bordagaray (above)
sported some unique whiskers.

1936 Leg up, ball out
Giants outfielder Mel Ott
employed a very unique batting
style, lifting one leg as he made
his stride. It was effective,
however–Ott slugged 511 career
home runs.

1936 First of four
Joe DiMaggio slides in ahead
of the tag during a play in the
World Series. The Yankees' victory
in six games was the first of their
four consecutive Series titles.

1936 Bashing brothers
Wes and Rick Ferrell (*left*) formed one of baseball's most unique duos for the Red Sox. They're the only brothers to homer while playing pitcher and catcher in the same game.

1936 Ol' Diz
The classic story about Cardinals ace Dizzy Dean (*above*)? After being beaned, Dean reported, "X-rays of my head revealed nothing."

1930s

1936 Desert ball
In the arid lands of Rimrock in western Oregon, residents of a Resettlement Administration camp take a break to get in a game in this Farm Security Administration photo by Arthur Rothstein.

1930s

1937 The Iron Horse swings
During a spring training game in Florida, Lou Gehrig shows the powerful swing that helped him amass 493 career home runs.

1930s

1937 On the air
Before gaining fame as an actor, and long before his days in politics, Ronald Reagan was a baseball radio broadcaster (*above*).

1937 Hey, Yankees!
As manager of the Yankees from 1931 to 1946, Joe McCarthy was blessed with talented players, and he guided them to a .614 winning percentage, a career best for managers.

1938 King Carl
Lefthander Carl Hubbell (*left*) rode an almost unhittable screwball to Major League success. With the New York Giants, he was among the top pitchers of the 1930s, leading the N.L. three times each in wins and ERA.

1938 Fans loved him
With Ruth and Gehrig gone or going by the late 1930s, "Joltin' Joe" DiMaggio (*above*), the "Yankee Clipper," became the fans' favorite.

1938 Singin' Dodgers
Babe Ruth, then a coach for Brooklyn, joined Tuck Stainback, Buddy Hassett, and Kiki Cuyler in some pregame musical hijinks (*following pages*).

1930s

1938 Six-pack for Hank
Detroit first baseman Hank Greenberg
(*above*) was one of baseball's greatest
sluggers, one of the first national
Jewish sports heroes, and one of the
first baseball players to join the Army
as World War II neared. In 1938,
Greenberg came close to Babe Ruth's
mark of 60 homers, with 58.

1939 Schnozz
As famous for his stunning lack of
foot speed as for his most prominent
facial feature, Ernie Lombardi (*right*)
was nevertheless one of baseball's
best-hitting catchers. In 1942, he
became the first catcher to lead his
league in batting.

1930s

1938 Watch out for the cows
During her work for the Depression-created Farm
Security Administration, famed photographer
Dorothea Lange captured scenes of baseball
Americana, like these baseball-playing farmers
near Mountain Home, Arkansas.

1939 Hanging out after the game
Lange photographed this general
store-cum-postgame locker room near
Chapel Hill, North Carolina.

1939 The other All-Stars
Homestead Grays catcher and legendary
slugger Josh Gibson (back row, third
from right) was among the baseball
luminaries that gathered at the Negro
League East-West All-Star game in
Chicago's Comiskey Park.

1939 Welcome to the club
Here are (almost) all the living members
of the Hall of Fame present at the
dedication of the Hall's new building.
Back row: Honus Wagner, Grover
Cleveland Alexander, Tris Speaker,
Napoleon Lajoie, George Sisler, Walter
Johnson; front row: Eddie Collins, Babe
Ruth, Connie Mack, Cy Young. Missing
from the photo was Ty Cobb.

1939 No, we were the lucky ones
Lou Gehrig pauses to compose himself
during the July 4, 1939, ceremonies
honoring him at Yankee Stadium.
Diagnosed a month before with ALS,
the disease that today bears his name,
Gehrig memorably called himself "the
luckiest man on the face of the earth,"
while thanking his teammates, fans, and
baseball itself.

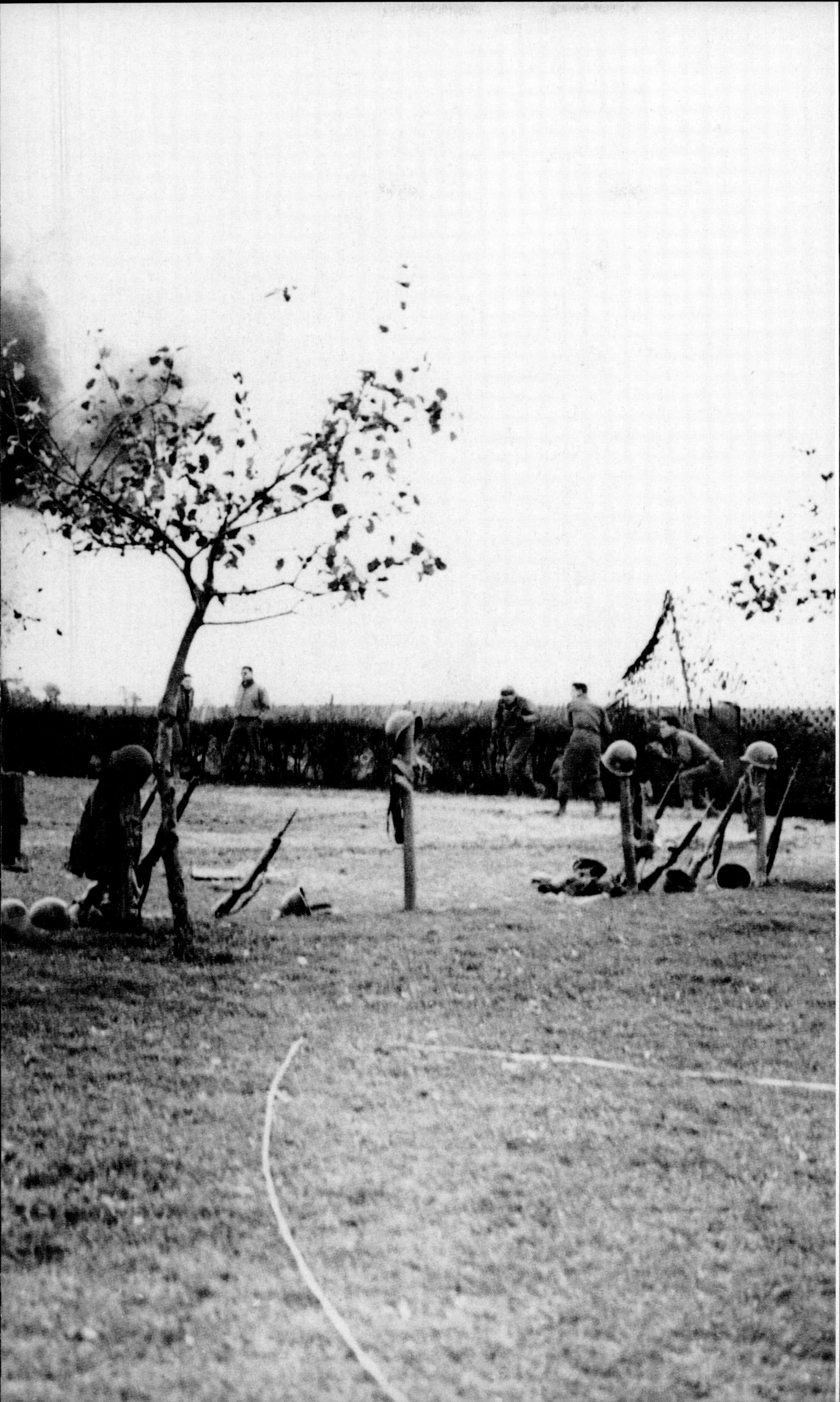

1940s

1940s
Baseball and WW II

1941 Another uniform
Phillies pitcher Hugh Mulcahy (*above*) shows that he can pitch in his U.S. Army uniform, too. Mulcahy was one of hundreds of Major Leaguers who joined various branches of the armed services.

1942 One for the boys
Joe DiMaggio (*left*) signs autographs for soldiers at Fort Dix, New Jersey, prior to an exhibition game.

1945 Baseball booms
(*Previous pages*) U.S. soldiers in North Africa ignore enemy shells to focus on a game.

During the first half of the 1940s, the world was turned upside down. By the end of the 1940s, the same thing happened to baseball.

On the field, the decade started with a bang, as the 1941 season featured two of baseball's most remarkable hitting achievements: Joe DiMaggio's 56-game hitting streak and Ted Williams's .406 batting average, the last to top .400 in the century. Off the field, of course, 1941 is remembered for a different sort of bang.

By the beginning of 1942, America was engulfed in World War II. There was talk of cancelling the Major League season that year and for the duration of the war.

But President Franklin Roosevelt intervened to keep the games going. In January, 1942, he wrote to Commissioner Kenesaw Landis, asking that the games go on. No other sport received similar presidential dispensation.

The games went on, but they often were played well below previous levels of skill. Hundreds of Major League players enlisted or left their teams to serve in the war. Stars such as Williams, DiMaggio, and Bob Feller left the game to serve in the armed forces. The minor leagues were decimated as thousands of their players headed overseas to fight. Minor leagues folded, teams suspended play, and the talent level slumped dramatically.

Then as the war ended, another shattering event hit baseball, an event that was long, long overdue.

In 1945, Jackie Robinson, a four-sport star at UCLA, a former Army officer, and a top player in the Negro Leagues, signed to play in the Brooklyn Dodgers organization. Two years later, he became the first African-American to play in the Major Leagues in the 1900s, smashing forever the heinous "color line" that had separated generations of great athletes from playing with the best of the best. Robinson, and the many other black players that soon joined the Majors, helped revolutionize the game . . . and in many ways, the nation.

1940s

1940 Still playing apart
Though its rosters were just as affected by the war as were those of the Major Leagues, the Negro Leagues had banner seasons in the early 1940s. The increase in production and employment gave many fans, notably black fans, more money and time to come out to the ballpark. By the end of the war, salaries for players were at their highest levels.

225

1940s

1940 Old Double X
Red Sox first baseman Jimmie Foxx
(*previous pages*) slugs his 495th
career home run (a game-winner
in this August 16 contest), passing
Lou Gehrig on the all-time list.
Foxx finished his career with
534 homers.

1941 The streak goes on
Joe DiMaggio (*right*) demonstrates
the picture-perfect stroke that
would help him create one of
baseball's enduring records—his
amazing streak of 56 consecutive
games with a hit. This hit came in
game number 39 of the streak.

1940s

1941 Say it ain't so
In New York, young fans, gloves in
hand, pay their respects to Lou Gehrig,
who died on June 3 of ALS.

1941 Play time
Recess at this homestead school in
Dailey, West Virginia, meant baseball.

1941 We pledge allegiance . . .
Far from the turmoil building in
Europe, patriotic players and fans at a
county fair game in Vale, Oregon,
stand at attention while listening via
radio to U.S. Chief Justice Harlan Stone
recite the pledge of allegiance. Their
duty done, it was on with the game.

1941 Teddy Ballgame goes yard
Ted Williams crosses the plate after his game-winning, three-run home run in the All-Star Game. Williams later called the blast one of the highlights of his career. Joe DiMaggio (5) greets him at the plate along with coach Marv Shea.

1941 Someday . . .
A future player watches the action in
Vale, Oregon. Does he dream of being
out there one day?

1942 Green uniforms
As America's armed forces trained for war, they often took time out to play a little ball (*above*), though they didn't always have time to change from one uniform to the other.

1942 Monumental game
The Washington Monument in Washington, D.C., towers above a weekend recreational game.

1940s

1942 Cooper in pinstripes
Actor Gary Cooper, as Yankee hero
Lou Gehrig, crosses the plate in this
still from the classic baseball movie
Pride of the Yankees.

1940s

1942 On location
Taking the game to the soldiers in the field, the members of the Army Air Force team pause to pose between games.

1940s

1947 No Madonnas here
Inspired by a dearth of male players during World War II, the All-American Girls Professional Baseball League (*above*) brought pro baseball to Midwestern towns like Racine, South Bend, and Kenosha. The league lasted until 1955, and was immortalized in the 1992 movie (starring Madonna, among others), *A League of Their Own*.

1947 Babe meets Bush
(*right*) Former president George Bush (far right), then a Yale first baseman, accepts a manuscript from a slightly more famous baseball man, Babe Ruth. The book was a gift to the Yale library.

1948 Happy . . . but not for long
A joyous Warren Spahn (*center*) celebrates the Boston Braves' win in Game 5 of the 1948 World Series. Spahn pitched 5 2/3 innings of one-hit relief to clinch Boston's 11-5 win. But the next day, the Cleveland Indians won Game 6 and the Series.

1948 Their hero
Just two months before his death from throat cancer, Babe Ruth spends some time with the fans to whom he was closest throughout his life: the kids.

1940s

1948 Goodbye, Babe

In one of the most famous photographs in baseball history, Nat Fein captured this moving image of Babe Ruth on the occasion of Babe Ruth Day, just three months before Babe's death of throat cancer. Leaning on a borrowed bat, Ruth basked one more time in the cheers he knew better than any other ballplayer.

1949 The Perfesser prophesies
Yankees manager Casey Stengel had a lot to look forward to: This season, his team began a string of five straight World Series titles.

1949 The Scooter
Shortstop Phil Rizzuto (throwing) was a key part of the Yankees' championship binge. He later was the team's long-time broadcaster.

1949 World Series con salsa
Since 1949, with the exception of 1961 to 1969 and 1981, the top teams in Latin America have met in the Caribbean World Series. This photograph (*left*) shows action from the first Series, held in Cuba and won by the host nation's Almendares team.

1946 Viva el béisbol!
South of the border in Mexico (*above*), baseball continued to rival soccer as the most popular sport. Major Leaguers often made their way south to keep their game sharp in the offseason by playing in very competitive winter leagues.

1940s

1949 Smile, team
The National League champion
Brooklyn Dodgers (*right*) pose
for a team picture before falling
once again to the Yankees
(*previous pages*) in the
World Series.

1949 Follow the bouncing ball
Dodgers catcher Roy Campanella
can't handle the throw (*following
pages*) and Gene Woodling of the
Yankees slides in safely during the
Yankees World Series victory. This
interborough battle was the
second of six World Series the
two teams would play from 1947
to 1956.

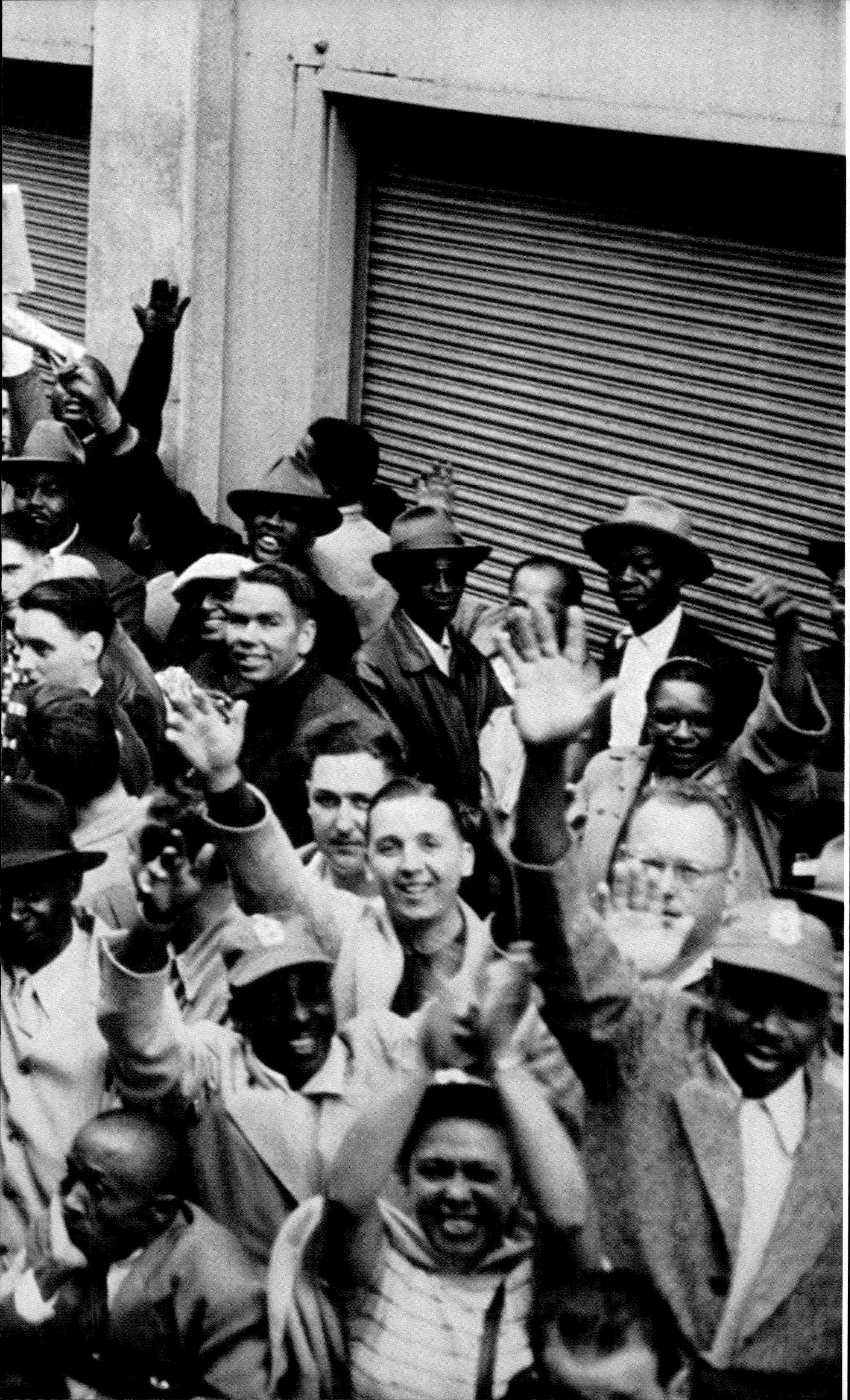

1950s

1950s
New York, New York

For the first eight seasons of the 1950s, New York was the center of the baseball world. For the last two, the city symbolized the game turning from the past to the future.

Though the city had long been home to three Major League teams–the New York Yankees of the American League and the New York Giants and Brooklyn Dodgers of the National League–in the 1950s, all three teams jointly reached new heights and their ongoing rivalries energized the baseball world. New York teams met each other in the World Series five times; at least one New York team appeared in every Series from 1950 through 1958. The Yankees dominated the decade, winning six Championship titles. The Giants (1954) and the Dodgers (1955) captured one apiece.

Each of the three team's stars became household names in the wider baseball world, but were considered part of the family by their New York faithful. Mickey Mantle, Yogi Berra, Whitey Ford, and other Yankees formed one of baseball's greatest dynasties. In Brooklyn, Jackie Robinson continued his heroics, Duke Snider was the star slugger, and Pee Wee Reese the leader. The Giants boasted Willie Mays, who many still rate the greatest all-around baseball player of all time.

Thanks to the growing popularity of television, the diamond soap operas starring these Big Apple heroes played out to a wider audience than ever before. Fans around the country learned the faces behind the stats better than ever.

Then, in one faith-shattering year, it was all over. In 1958, the holy trinity of New York baseball was broken when the Dodgers moved to–gasp– Los Angeles, and the Giants to San Francisco. They became the first Major League teams west of St. Louis.

The 1950s were a great ride for baseball, a ride that ended not with a sudden jolt, but with the first step on an even bigger ride.

1950s

1950 "Yer out!"
More than 68,000 fans packed a red-white-and-blue bunting-bedecked Yankee Stadium for Game 4 of the 1950 World Series. Umpire Charles Berry makes the call as Yankees catcher Yogi Berra tags out Philadelphia's Granny Hamner. The Yankees won the game 5-2, clinching the first of their six world championships in the 1950s.

1950 Domo arigato, Joe
Joe DiMaggio gives some pointers to Japanese players during an off-season tour that also visited U.S. military bases in Asia.

1950s

1950 Star power

Bob Hope (*above*, seated left) and Jack Benny (far right) join Cleveland Indians manager Lou Boudreau for a spring training game in Florida. Benny looks like he's all set to fight for a foul ball.

1950 The Whiz Kids

Pitcher Robin Roberts (*right*) led the Philadelphia Phillies, nicknamed "The Whiz Kids," into the 1950 World Series, the team's first postseason appearance since 1915. However, the mighty Yankees swept the Phils.

1950s

1951 World's smallest player
St. Louis Browns owner Bill Veeck pulled off baseball's most outrageous publicity stunt when he hired–with a legal, one-day baseball contract–midget Eddie Gaedel. Wearing number 1/8, Gaedel, not surprisingly, walked in his only plate appearance.

c.1950s Small name, big man
Shortstop Pee Wee Reese (*right*) was the emotional heart of the Brooklyn Dodgers, helping them win six N.L. pennants from 1947 to 1956. Reese's leadership also was instrumental in guiding teammates and opponents in accepting Jackie Robinson.

1950 The Kid
After leading the A.L. in 1949 in runs, home runs, RBI, slugging percentage, and walks, among other things, Ted Williams suffered an arm injury in the 1950 All-Star game. Until surgery was successfully completed, there were fears that Williams's great career was over.

1951 The act of pitching
(*right*) That's famed Cleveland pitcher Bob Lemon on the left, but who is that on the right? Why, none other than actor and future president Ronald Reagan, getting some tips from Lemon before starring in a movie about Hall of Fame pitcher Grover Cleveland Alexander.

1951 New York's new hero
DiMaggio's last year with the Yankees was Mickey Mantle's first (*left*). With unmatched speed and awesome power from both sides of the plate, "The Mick" carried the Yankees to dominance in the 1950s.

1951 A pair of aces
St. Louis's Stan Musial (no. 6) congratulates Pittsburgh's Ralph Kiner after Kiner's eighth-inning home run in the All-Star Game (left). Kiner is one of baseball's most unheralded sluggers; he led the N.L. in homers a record seven consecutive seasons (1946 to 1952).

1951 Working on the stick
There's no real proof that the act of "boning the bat," which supposedly tightened up the grain and made it harder, improved one's hitting. But who is going to argue with Joe DiMaggio, a lifetime .325 hitter? Joltin' Joe retired after the 1951 season.

1950s

1951 Shot heard 'round the world
Probably the most famous home run in baseball
history was this shot into the leftfield seats at
the Polo Grounds by Bobby Thomson of the
New York Giants. Made more famous by Russ
Hodges' apoplectic–yet correct–radio call, "The
Giants win the pennant!" the homer won the
third game of a special playoff series forced
when the Giants and the Brooklyn Dodgers tied
after the regular season.

1951 Way to go, Bobby!
Thomson (under hand at center) was the center
of attention as he wrapped up his jig-dancing
way around the bases. The Giants' win capped
off a tremendous stretch drive that included a
16-game winning streak that helped them
come from far off the pace to tie Brooklyn.

1952 Private Willie Mays
The "Say-Hey Kid" (*left*) trades in his spikes for military boots after being drafted. The Giants lost Mays for most of 1952 and all of 1953.

1952 Teddy Airplane
Already a decorated pilot from his World War II service, Ted Williams (*above*) returned to the air, this time in jet planes during the Korean War. Williams again served with distinction and once walked away from the crash of his burning jet.

1950s

1952 Casey at the beach
During spring training in Florida, Yankees manager Casey Stengel is surrounded by autograph-seeking kids.

1950s

1952 It's a baseball town
Yankee Stadium in the Bronx (top) and
the Polo Grounds in Manhattan (bottom)
were close enough that fans could see
one park from the other. The 1950s
became the last hurrah for New York as
the home of three Major League teams:
The Yankees, the Giants, and the
Dodgers at Ebbets Field in Brooklyn.

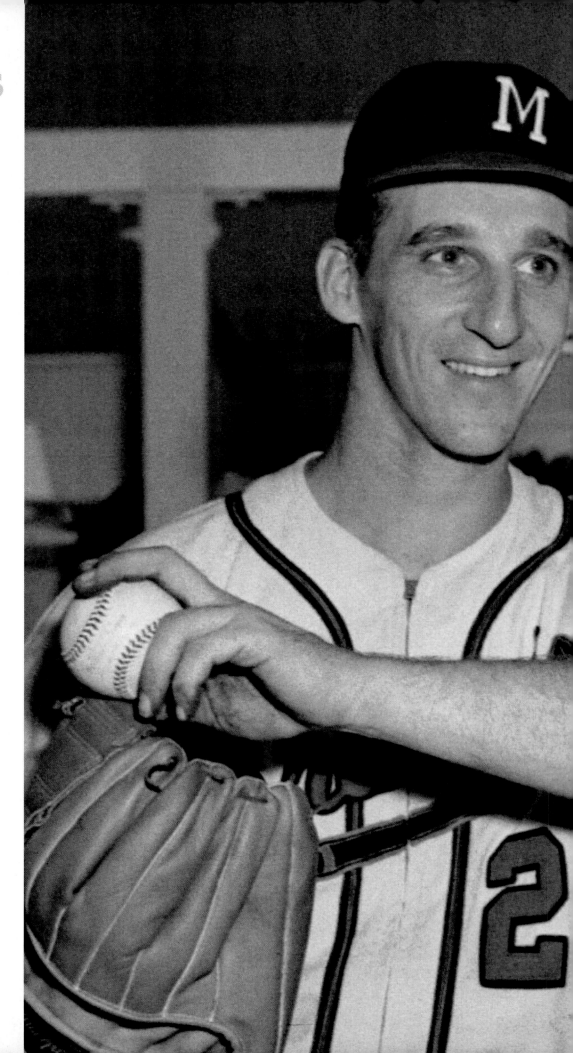

1950s

1953 Perfect peg, perfect play
(*previous pages*) After taking a throw from outfiedler Carl Furillo, Dodgers catcher Roy Campanella tags out the Giants' Jim Hearn to save a run.

1953 Feel that muscle!
For the young son of a team-mate, Braves pitcher Warren Spahn shows off the arm that would eventually help him win more games (363) than any other lefthander in baseball history.

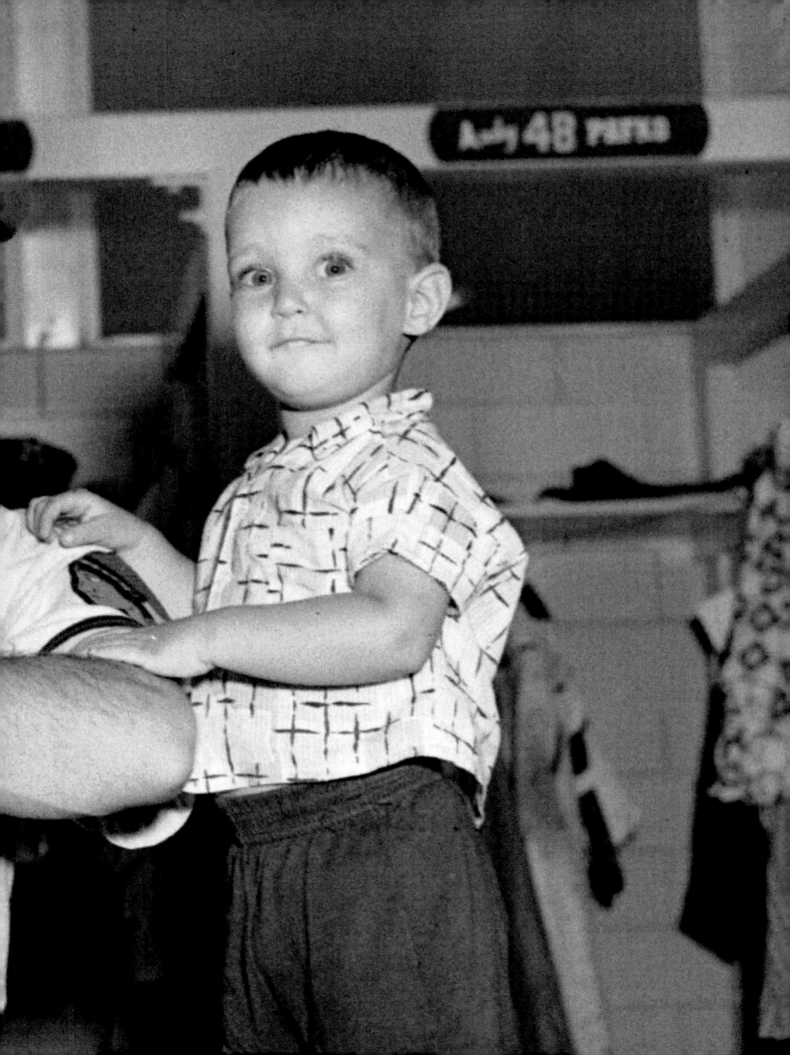

1950s

1954 Viva Willie!
Like several other Major Leaguers, Willie Mays (*above*) kept in shape during the winter by playing in Latin America. Here Mays slides into third while playing for the Santurce Cangrejeros (Crabbers) in Puerto Rico.

1954 The Catch
Willie Mays (*following pages*) first tracks down and then fires home this long drive off the bat of Vic Wertz in Game 1 of the 1954 World Series. The stunning catch-and-throw by a perennial Gold Glover is regarded as one of the greatest defensive plays in baseball history.

1954 Fractured fairy tale
Though a happy couple here just after their wedding in January (*right*), movie goddess Marilyn Monroe and baseball legend Joe DiMaggio would be divorced by October.

1954 Stan the Man
By the mid-1950s, Stan Musial (*above*) was among the most-feared hitters in the National League. A seven-time batting champion and three-time MVP, he also appeared in a record 24 All-Star games.

1954 Welcome home, Ted
Showing no letdown from his time away from baseball while flying jet planes in the Korean War, Ted Williams (*right*) batted no less than .345 in each of the first four full seasons (1954 to 1958) after his return.

.

1954 The coach and the kid
Under the tutelage of Casey Stengel,
Mickey Mantle (*left*) became one of
baseball's biggest stars.

1955 Campy crushes
Dodgers catcher Roy Campanella
(*above*) gets another hit on the
way to his third MVP award in the
Dodgers' championship season.

1950s

1955 Next year finally came
In the sixth inning of Game 7
of the World Series, Brooklyn's
Sandy Amoros makes an historic,
game-saving catch of a drive
by the Yankees' Yogi Berra. The
miracle grab helped the Dodgers
win their first World Series.

1955 Sweet taste of success
Doused in celebratory beer, Duke
Snider and Don Newcombe revel in
Brooklyn's World Series victory. After
decades of playing second fiddle to
the Yankees, the Dodgers finally
reached the top.

315

1956 Just getting started
Chicago White Sox outfielder Minnie Minoso (*left*) would become baseball's ageless wonder. He recorded at-bats in every decade from the 1940s to 1980s, including getting a hit in 1976 at the age of 54.

1950s Away from the spotlight
Baseball was the game for more than just Major Leaguers. All sorts of organizations, such as these Kiwanis (*above*), sponsored or put together teams throughout America.

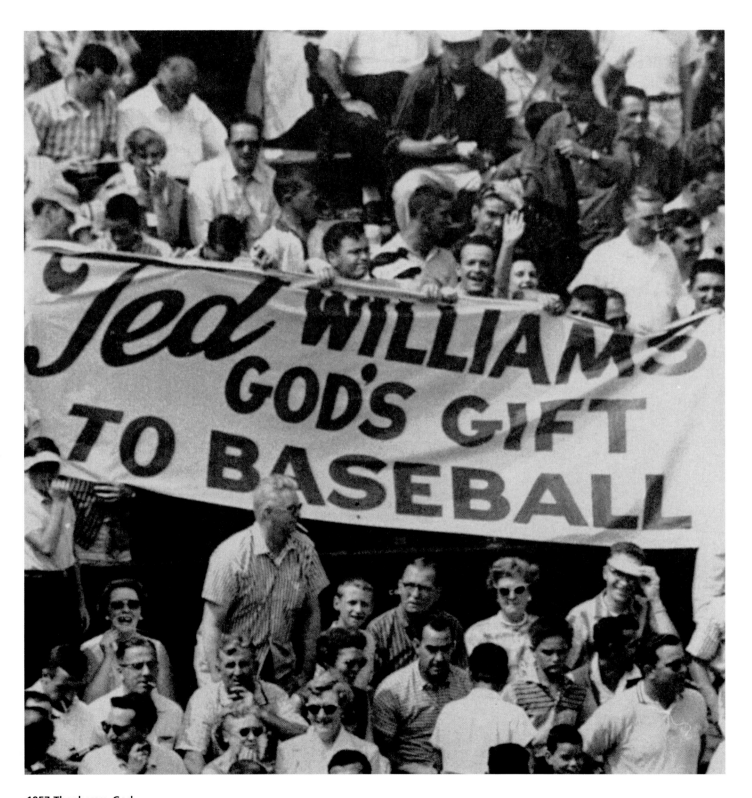

1957 Thank you, God
Boston fans, always a fickle lot toward their heroes, on this day saluted Williams, on his way to another batting championship.

1950s

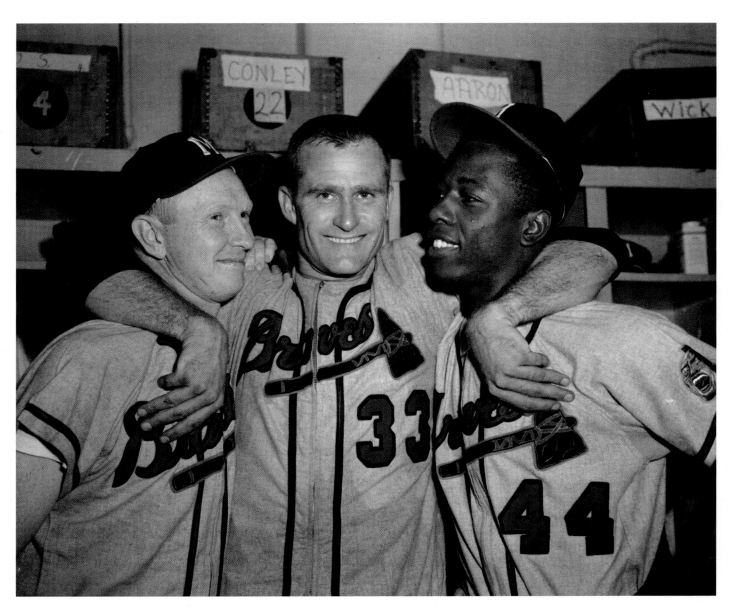

1957 Sweet Lew
Milwaukee Braves pitcher Lew Burdette joins teammates Red Schoendienst and Hank Aaron in celebrating their team's seven-game World Series triumph over the Yankees. Burdette's three victories and 0.67 ERA played a huge hand in the championship.

1957 O happy day!
Fans in Los Angeles react with glee to
the news that Major League Baseball is
finally coming to their town. The
Dodgers, to the stunned sadness of
their Brooklyn fans, announced plans to
begin playing in sunny LA beginning in
the 1958 season.

1950s

1958 Welcome to your new home
Willie Mays and friend watch as
movers help the Mays' family make
San Francisco their new home. Like
the Dodgers, the Giants moved West
following the 1957 season.

332

1950s

1958 Finally . . . baseball

This ticker-tape parade through San Francisco (*above*) awaited the Giants when they arrived in their new home. Along with the Dodgers, they were the first Major League teams west of the Mississippi.

1958 Still swingin'

Stan Musial (*following pages*) becomes the eighth man to reach 3,000 hits in a career with this pinch-hit double against the White Sox. Musial finished his illustrious career as the all-time N.L. leader in hits.

1959 So close . . . and yet so far
Pittsburgh pitcher Harvey Haddix (*above*)
pitched 12 perfect innings against
Milwaukee, but neither team scored
until the 13th, when two hits finally did
the unlucky Haddix, and the Pirates, in.

1959 Home run champ
Braves slugger Eddie Mathews (*right*)
won the home run title this season with
46 round-trippers. Teaming with Hank
Aaron, he helped form the Major's most
devastating home run duo.

1960s

1960s
Suddenly The Sixties

The 1960s were a tumultuous time for many Americans, and baseball was not insulated from the change and uncertainty that gripped the nation.

On the field, the Yankees began the decade by playing in five consecutive World Series, winning two. The Bronx Bombers were so power-laden that not one, but two, players launched an assault on Babe Ruth's long-standing, single-season home run record in 1961. Mickey Mantle fell off the pace late in the season, but Roger Maris' sixty-first homer came on the final day and eclipsed Ruth's record–though the Commissioner, Ford Frick, ruled that the mark would be accompanied by an asterisk because Maris' season was eight games longer than Ruth's.

The offensive barrage was so prevalent throughout both leagues that the Major Leagues adopted a bigger strike zone midway through the decade, causing a wild pendulum swing that shifted power back to the pitchers. By 1968, the aggregate major-league ERA was below 3.00. That season, St. Louis' Bob Gibson had 13 shutouts and a miniscule ERA of 1.12. Boston's Carl Yastrzemski led the A.L. with a batting average of just .301, the lowest league-leading mark in history. The strike zone was reduced and the pitching mound lowered in 1969.

That season, the Miracle Mets won the World Series. The Mets burst onto the scene as an expansion team in 1962–they were one of four new franchises in the decade–and promptly lost 120 of 162 games. But they captured the hearts of New York fans accustomed to the flawless Yankees. And in 1969, the first year that both leagues were split into divisions, the Mets won the N.L. East. They went on to beat the Atlanta Braves to capture the pennant, then stunned the Baltimore Orioles in the World Series.

Off the field, baseball dug in at the end of the decade for a watershed challenge to its long-standing reserve clause by Cardinals outfielder Curt Flood.

1960s

1960 Mr. Nice Guy, too
Ernie Banks was known as "Mr. Cub" for most of his Hall of Fame career in Chicago. Originally a slugging shortstop, he later played first base, while also finding time to play with Chicago's young fans.

1960 What a way to go
Head famously bowed, cap untipped,
Ted Williams finishes up his last
hit . . . fittingly, a home run, the 521st
of his amazing career. Writer John
Updike later captured the moment with
his essay, "Hub Fans Bid Kid Adieu."

1960s

1960 Future Texas Ranger?
L.A. Dodgers pitcher Don Drysdale
(*above*) fell under the spell of nearby
Hollywood when he and fellow pitcher
Sandy Koufax appeared in a TV western.

1960 Driving a Ford
The talented left arm of Whitey Ford
(*right*) took the Yankees on many an
October drive. A member of 11 Yankee
pennant winners, he holds several
World Series pitching records.

1960s

1961 Baby Bull
Puerto Rican star Orlando Cepeda
(*above*) was the first Giants player
to emerge as a star on the West
Coast. He led the N.L. with 46
home runs and 142 RBI. He also
topped .300 six times in his Hall
of Fame career.

1961 Say Hey's safe
Willie Mays (*right*) was the first
player to both hit 300 home runs
(he would end his career with
660, third-most all-time) and steal
300 bases, combining power and
speed as no other player before
and only a few since.

1961 Twice as powerful
Mickey Mantle shows off half of his arsenal with this left-handed swing. Mantle hit more home runs than any other switch-hitter in baseball history. Fifty-four of his career total of 565 dingers came in the monumental summer of 1961, when a knee injury in September knocked him out of a race with Roger Maris toward the magic mark of 60.

1961 He did it
With this swing, Roger Maris (*left*) broke Babe Ruth's seemingly unbreakable record of 60 home runs in one season. Maris' record of 61 would stand until 1998.

1961 Sigh of relief
Maris' face, as seen here retrieving the 61st home run ball from young Sal Durante, who wrestled it to the ground in the bleachers, betrays immense relief mixed with his happiness. At last, the pressure was off.

1960s

1962 Generalissimo Béisbol
A hard-throwing righthander before he took a hard left turn politically, Cuban leader Fidel Castro (*above*) was once scouted by the Yankees in the 1950s.

1962 He kept going and going . . .
Though he didn't reach the Majors until 1952 when he was 28, World War II veteran Hoyt Wilhelm (*right*) used a baffling knuckleball until he was 48, pitching in a then-record 1,071 games.

1962 Time for aspirin
As the eminently quotable manager of the New York Mets' hapless expansion team, veteran baseball man Casey Stengel (left) needed all the help he could get.

1962 Angeles Arms
The Dodgers were helped to three N.L. pennants by a great crew of pitchers, (*above*) including Don Drysdale, Pete Richert, Stan Williams, Sandy Koufax, and Johnny Podres.

1962 Wonderful Wills
Maury Wills kicks up a cloud of
Dodger Stadium dust while racking up
the last of his amazing 104 stolen
bases, more than twice as many as any
other N.L. player had had since 1923.

1962 Now listen up
Casey Stengel goes over the fine
points with his Mets charges. Though
Stengel won five World Series with
the Yankees, he couldn't nudge the
Mets into the first division.

1962 Washington righthander
John F. Kennedy continued the Presidential tradition of throwing out first balls, though he was really more of a touch football man.

1963 A fearsome sight
Though his career really only peaked
for five seasons in the first half of the
1960s, Sandy Koufax, here pitching in
the 1963 World Series, is regarded as
one of the greatest pitchers ever.

1960s

1963 Across the pond
The Japanese professional leagues continued to flourish, as shown by this well-attended game at Tokyo's Korokuen Stadium.

371

1960s

1964 Another baseball King
Taking a break from his work for civil rights, Martin Luther King, Jr., shows his son Marty the finer points of baseball.

1960s

1964 The first Mr. October

Mickey Mantle (*above*) rounds the bases after one of his record 18 World Series home runs. This one, his record-setting 16th, was a walk-off homer, winning Game 3 of the 1964 Series.

1964 Commerce Comet caught

The next game, Mantle wasn't so lucky (*following pages*). He was picked off second base in Game 4, which the Cardinals won on their way to a seven-game Series championship.

373

1964 Hearty breakfast
Cardinals manager Red Schoendienst (*above*, left) dishes out some eggs to Stan Musial (third from left), then a Cardinals coach, and star pitcher Bob Gibson (right) during spring training.

1964 Lobbing one in
U.S. servicemen (*right*) engage some kids in a game during their tour of duty in the Dominican Republic. By the 1990s, the island nation would produce more Major Leaguers than any other nation outside the U.S.

1960s

1965 Don't look back . . .
Can that really be Satchel Paige,
firing in another heater at the alleged
age of 59? Ol' Satch came out of
retirement to show that he still had
the stuff, starting one game for the
Kansas City Royals.

1965 Perfection
Sandy Koufax capped off his
remarkable career with the eighth
perfect game in baseball history, a
1-0 defeat of the Cubs. It was also
Koufax's fourth no-hitter.

1960s

1965 East meets West
Willie Mays passes on some tips on big-league hitters to Masanori Murakami, the first Japanese-born player in the Majors. He pitched for the Giants in 1964 to 1965.

1965 Gimme a J . . .
Teams in Japan melded their culture
with baseball traditions, creating
such unique entertainments as these
kimono-clad cheerleaders atop a
Japan League dugout.

1965 A climbing Rose
Reds second baseman Pete Rose gets some serious air while snagging this errant throw. Rose, who would become baseball's all-time hits leader, played every infield position but short-stop, as well as outfield, during his long career.

1960s

1965 Spahn's last hurrah
Well, almost. Warren Spahn, the
all-time winningest left-hander, spent
his final season going 4-12 with the
Mets and 3-4 with the Giants.

1966 One in a million
A pitcher hitting a grand slam is very, very rare. A pitcher hitting two in one game is rarer still. But Atlanta pitcher Tony Cloninger accomplished the feat, driving in nine runs in a game in 1966.

1966 In with the new . . .
In an exhibition game, Mickey
Mantle (left) christened the new
Houston Astrodome with its first
home run. The 'Dome is baseball's
first indoor stadium.

1966 . . . out with the old
The Braves' franchise moved to
Atlanta in 1966. Eddie Matthews (41)
and Hank Aaron leave Milwaukee's
County Stadium for the last time in
September 1965 (*above*).

1960s

1966 A flock of Robinsons
Brooks (left) and Frank Robinson led
the Baltimore Orioles to a 1966 World
Series triumph. Brooks was perhaps
the finest-fielding third baseman ever.

1966 Crowning glory
Frank Robinson, meanwhile, swung a
monstrous bat. He led the A.L. in
1966 with a .316 average, 49 homers,
and 122 RBI, becoming the first A.L.
player to win the Triple Crown since
Mickey Mantle in 1956.

1966 Big Bird

Orioles pitcher Jim Palmer (*left*) demonstrates the form that helped him throw a 4-hit shutout in Game 2 of the 1966 World Series, in which Baltimore swept the Dodgers.

1966 The Big A

The Los Angeles Angels became the California Angels in 1966 when they moved into Anaheim Stadium (*above*). The "Big A" sign in left field quickly became one of baseball's most recognizable symbols.

1960s

1967 A Little League dream . . .
In Williamsport, Pennsylvania, dreams
come true at the Little League World
Series (*above*). These young players from
Tokyo went home as world champs.

1967 . . . and an impossible one
The last man to win the Triple Crown, Red Sox
slugger Carl Yastrzemski (*right*), led Boston to
an improbable berth in the 1967 World Series.
Though he homers here in Game 2, he wasn't
enough, and the Cardinals won the title.

1960s

1968 Getting closer . . .
Hank Aaron (*left*) hit only 29 home runs this season. But in 1969, he began a home run binge, clubbing more than 200 homers in the next five seasons to pull within one of Babe Ruth going into the 1974 season.

1968 Meet you at home
Tigers catcher Bill Freehan gets the better of this collision with Lou Brock during the 1968 World Series (*right*). Brock was out on this play, and the Tigers were soon to become world champions.

1968 Oh, to be a kid again
At the end of his great career, Roger Maris (*below*) helped the Cardinals win three N.L. pennants. Here he watches as his sons and a friend enjoy a game of catch in the St. Louis locker room.

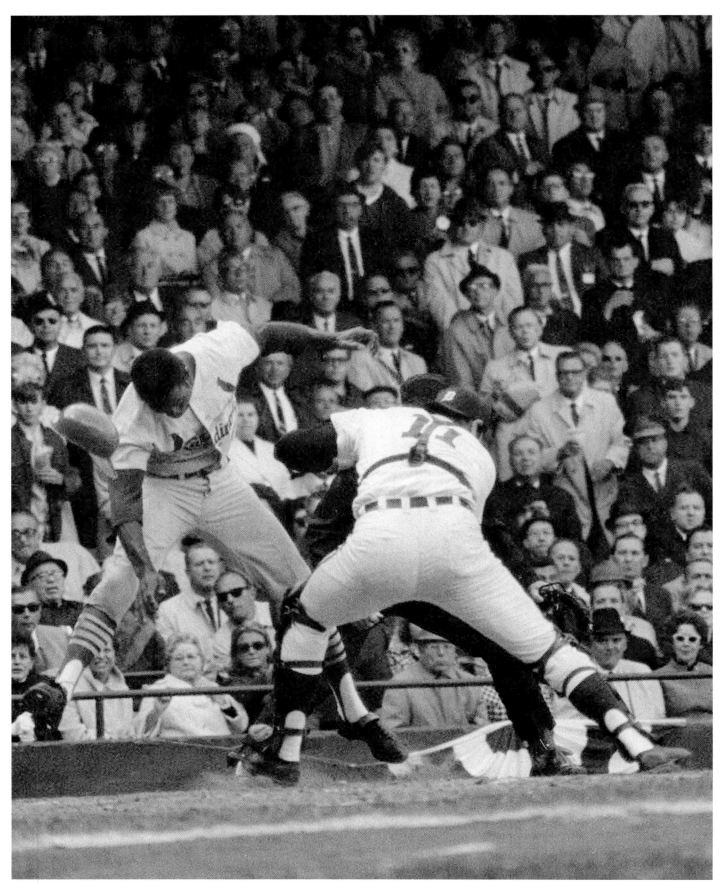

1968 Another over there
Baseball had traveled with American soldiers to Europe, Latin America, Japan, Africa, and elsewhere. In the 1960s, it went to Vietnam (*left*).

1968 The last one
Denny McClain (*above*) used a fierce fastball, a bigger strike zone, and a championship Tigers team to post a 31-6 record. He is the last pitcher to reach 30 wins in one season.

401

1969 What a right wing
Secretary of State Henry Kissinger (*above*, in the dark blue suit) fired out a first pitch at a Washington Senators' game, joined by baseball Commissioner Bowie Kuhn.

1969 Two champs
Future home run champ Hank Aaron (*left*) turns fan as he asks boxing great and fellow future sports legend Muhammad Ali for an autograph.

1969 Collapsible Cubs
Though Ron Santo (*right*) was a fine third baseman for the Chicago Cubs, he wasn't enough to keep them from losing eight in a row in September to miss out on a division title.

1960s

1969 Being kids . . .
(*above*) The ball is not supposed to fit
through the protective mesh screen,
but that doesn't stop these determined
youngsters from giving it a "pry."

1969 . . . acting like kids
Celebrating the "Amazin' Mets" World
Series triumph, two New York businessmen
(*right*) kick up their heels amid the residue
of the ticker tape parade.

1970s

1970s
The Polyester Seventies

After being traded from the St. Louis Cardinals to the Philadelphia Phillies after the 1969 season, then refusing to report to his new club, veteran outfielder Curt Flood filed suit against Major League Baseball, challenging its long-standing reserve clause. Flood eventually lost the litigation, but he succeeded in focusing attention on the issue, and the labor landscape would change dramatically in the 1970s. By the middle of the decade, the era of free agency had begun, and player movement and salaries were on the rise.

Between the lines, the baseball world focused on Henry Aaron, who closed in on Babe Ruth's record of

714 career home runs. The Braves' slugger finished the 1973 season at 713, then tied the mark on his first swing of the 1974 season at Cincinnati on April 4. Four days later, Aaron belted number 715 off the Dodgers' Al Downing at Atlanta.

The World Series produced some magical moments in the seventies. Brooks Robinson carried the Orioles past the Reds in 1970 with dazzling defense at third base and a .429 average and two home runs at the plate. The Athletics won back-to-back-to-back titles from 1972 to 1974. Carlton Fisk's dramatic 12th-inning homer won Game 6 for the Red Sox in 1975, but the Reds came

from behind to win Game 7 the next day. And Reggie Jackson homered on three consecutive swings to put an exclamation point on the Yankees' win over the Dodgers in 1977.

The baseball world was stunned by the deaths of two of its brightest stars. Pirates outfielder Roberto Clemente, 38, who recorded his 3,000th hit late in the 1972 season, was killed that New Year's Eve in a plane crash. He was helping to bring relief supplies to the victims of a devastating earthquake in Nicaragua. In August, 1979, Yankees' captain and seven-time All-Star catcher Thurman Munson was killed while piloting a private plane on an off-day. He was just 32.

1970s

1970 Charlie Hustle
(right) Who says it's an exhibition game? The Reds' Pete Rose bowls over Oakland catcher Ray Fosse to score the winning run in the 12th inning of the All-Star Game at Cincinnati.

1970 Captain Concepcion
(below) Rookie shortstop Dave Concepcion joined the Reds, and three years later became captain of the Big Red Machine. He would win five Gold Gloves and earn eight All-Star nods.

1970s

1970 Pitch man
(above) Jim Palmer won 20 games for the Orioles, the first of his eight 20-win seasons in a nine-year span. He was the American League's Cy Young Award winner in 1973, 1975, and 1976.

1970 Gentle giant
(right) Washington's Frank Howard led the American League with 44 home runs, 126 RBI, and 132 walks, capping a three-year span in which he belted 136 round trippers.

1970s Birds of a feather
(opposite page) Baltimore had one of the American League's most successful franchises of the decade, winning five division titles, three pennants, and the 1970 World Series.

1970 Hammerin' Hank
Atlanta's Henry "Hank" Aaron continued his assault on baseball's record books, recording his 3,000th hit and belting his 600th career home run.

1970s

1970 Benchmark
(above) The Reds' Johnny Bench established offensive standards by which all catchers are judged. He led the National League with 45 homers and 148 RBI in 1970, the first of his two MVP seasons.

1970 Niekro's knuckler
Phil Niekro's trademark pitch, the knuckleball, enabled him to play until 1987, when he retired at age 48. He won 318 games in 24 seasons, most of them for the Atlanta Braves.

1971 The Original Bonds Man
(left) Bobby Bonds starred for the
Giants two decades before his son,
Barry, did. Bobby reached 30 homers
and 30 steals five times in his
14-year career.

1971 Two dozen
Ferguson Jenkins won 284 games in
his career, including 24 for the Cubs
in 1971, when he won the National
League's Cy Young Award.

1970s

1970s Good field, good hit
(*above*) Brooks Robinson became
a household name because of his
fielding, but the Orioles' third
baseman also hit 268 homers and
amassed 2,848 hits in his career.

1970s Pops
(*right*) Pittsburgh's Willie Stargell
averaged 30 home runs and 91 RBI
per season in the seventies. He was
N.L. Co-MVP in 1979, when the
Pirates won the World Series.

1970s

1970s Frequent rivals
(previous pages) Catcher Johnny Bench's Cincinnati Reds and Willie Stargell's Pittsburgh Pirates combined for 10 division titles in the 1970s and squared off three times in the postseason.

1972 Tragic ending
(above) Pirates' star Roberto Clemente was killed while delivering relief supplies for earthquake victims in Managua, Nicaragua, on New Year's Eve.

1970s Holy cow!
(right) It might be! It could be! It is! Harry Caray broadcasting from the bleachers. Caray called games for the Cardinals, A's, White Sox, and Cubs in his career.

1970s

1972 Start of a slump
(above) The American League is introduced prior to the All-Star Game in Atlanta. The squad lost the game, 4-3–the first of 11 consecutive A.L. defeats.

1972 Pudge
(left) Catcher Carlton Fisk broke into the Red Sox lineup and earned American League rookie of the year honors after batting .293 with 22 homers.

1972 Lone ace
(right) Steve Carlton, who went on to win 329 games in 24 major-league seasons, won 27 games for a Phillies' team that won only 59 all season.

1972 Power surge
(following pages) Gene Tenace sparked Oakland's victory over the Reds when he became the first player ever to homer in each of his first two at-bats in the World Series.

1970s Captain of the ship
(above) Shipping magnate George Steinbrenner took over the Yankees in 1973. New York went on to win back-to-back World Series in 1977 and 1978.

1973-75 Testing the waters
(right) Andy Messersmith won 53 games for the Dodgers, then became one of baseball's first big-name free agents and signed with Atlanta in 1976.

1973 Familiar sight
(left) Minnesota's Rod Carew follows through on a base hit. The seven-time batting champion had a career average of .328 in 19 Major League seasons.

1970s

1974 End of the chase
(*above*) Atlanta's Hank Aaron beams after his 715th career home run broke Babe Ruth's all-time record. Aaron would reach 755 homers before retiring after the 1976 season.

1974 Summer vacation
(*right*) Enigmatic Dick Allen led the American League with 32 home runs despite taking off much of the last month of the season.

1974 Leap year
Star slugger Reggie Jackson
helped carry the Oakland A's to
their third consecutive World
Series title.

1975 On again, off again
(above) Tempestuous Billy Martin served five stints as manager of the New York Yankees between 1975 and 1988.

1975 Run Producer
(right) Tony Perez flourished as an RBI man in the midst of the Reds' powerful lineup. In 1975, he drove in more than 100 runs for the sixth time in nine years.

1975 In between
(left) Gaylord Perry was traded to Texas three years after winning the Cy Young Award for the Indians. Three years later, he won the award again for San Diego.

1975 More to come

(left) Cincinnati's George Foster had a breakthrough season, belting 23 home runs. He would hit 121 over the next three years and tie a major-league record with three consecutive RBI titles.

1975 Groundbreaker

(right) Frank Robinson, an MVP in both leagues, became baseball's first black manager when he took over for Cleveland in 1975 while remaining an active player.

1975 Ryan's express

(below) Nolan Ryan is all smiles after throwing the fourth of his record seven no-hitters in a 1-0 victory over the Orioles.

1970s

1975 Home at last
(*previous pages*) Carlton Fisk stomps on home plate after his dramatic 12th-inning home run beat the Reds in Game 6 of the World Series. Cincinnati came from behind to win Game 7 the next day.

1976 Playing days
(*above*) Dusty Baker, who would go on to become a successful Major League manager, played for four teams in a 19-year career, mostly with the Braves and the Dodgers.

1976-77 Trophy collection
(*right*) Philadelphia's Steve Carlton posted back-to-back 20-win seasons, including 23 in 1977, when he won the second of his then-record four Cy Young Awards.

1970s

1976 Wrigley regular
(above) Billy Williams retired after amassing 2,711 hits and 426 home runs in 18 seasons. He was a fixture in Chicago, where he played 16 years with the Cubs before finishing with two seasons in Oakland.

1976 Baseball hero
(right) Los Angeles' Rick Monday slides into home. Monday became a national hero that season when he prevented two men from burning an American flag in the outfield at Dodger Stadium.

1976 The Bird
(left) Detroit's Mark Fidrych burst onto the scene with his unique quirks and enthusiasm for the game. He won 19 games and led the A.L. with a 2.34 ERA.

1976 Scouting report
(right) Youngsters in Canada eye their opponents before taking their turn on the field.

1976 Marine life
(below) The Marlins wouldn't join the National League for another two decades, but this dolphin was playing baseball in the mid-1970s.

1977 Mr. October
(left) Reggie Jackson cements his World Series legacy when he blasts his third home run of the Yankees' 8-4 victory over the Dodgers in the decisive Game 6.

1977 Junior's dad
(above) Ken Griffey, Sr., was a star in his own right during a 19-year career in which amassed 2,143 hits. He earned his second All-Star berth while with the Reds in 1977.

1970s

1977 All-stars

(above) The National League squad poses before the 1977 All-Star Game at Yankee Stadium in New York. The National League scored four times in the first inning en route to a 7-5 victory.

1977 Tom Terrific

(left) After a decade with the Mets, which included four 20-plus win seasons, Tom Seaver was dealt to the Reds in the middle of 1977 and won 14 of 17 games for the Reds the rest of the year.

1977 Stolen Base King

(right) Lou Brock steals a base to break Ty Cobb's record for career thefts. Brock retired in 1979 with 938 steals.

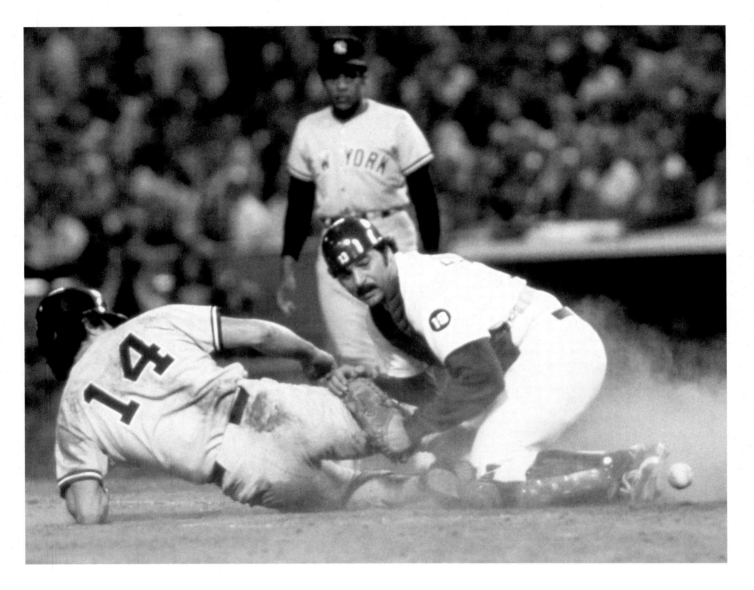

1978 Dazzling display
(left) The Yankees' Graig Nettles was
a power hitter who belted 390 career
home runs, but it was his flashy
fielding in Game 3 that helped turn
around the 1978 World Series.

1978 Safe at the plate
(above) Yankees outfielder Lou Piniella
kicks the ball away from Dodgers
catcher Joe Ferguson in the World
Series. New York won in six games
despite dropping Games 1 and 2.

1978 Rookie highlight
(*left*) The Dodgers' Bob Welch
delivers a pitch in the 1978 World
Series. The first-year hurler struck
out Reggie Jackson to save Game 2,
but the Yankees won in six.

1979 Milestone year
(*above*) Boston's Carl Yastrzemski
surpassed 3,000 hits and 400 home
runs. He retired in 1983 with 3,419
hits and 452 homers in a storied
23-year career.

1979 Monster seasons

(left) Jim Rice capped a huge three-year run in which he batted .320 with 124 home runs, 383 RBI, and 620 hits for the Red Sox. He was the A.L. MVP in 1978.

1979 Little Joe

(right) Joe Morgan ended an eight-year stretch as the Reds' second baseman, a span in which he recorded more than 100 walks and 100 runs in six seasons and made the All-Star team each year.

1979 All part of the fun

(below) Twins fans patiently wait for a chance to get their favorite star's autograph before a game in Minneapolis.

1979 Warmup act
(above) The Famous Chicken helps Gary Carter warm up a National League pitcher at baseball's 50th All-Star Game in Seattle.

1979 A slick fielder, too
(right) Cardinals' first baseman Keith Hernandez shared the MVP Award after leading the National League in batting average, runs, doubles, and on-base percentage.

1979 A heartbreaking loss
(left) Catcher Thurman Munson, the Yankees' popular captain and a seven-time All-Star, was killed at 32 when piloting a small plane that crashed on August 2.

1970s

1979 Giant stroke
(above) Legendary Japanese slugger
Sadaharu Oh takes batting practice.
Oh belted 868 home runs for Japan's
Yomiuri Giants from 1959 to 1981.

1979 Billy Ball
(right) Billy Martin returned in July to
manage the Yankees and harass
umpires. One year later, Martin was
hired by Oakland, and helped revive
the moribund A's.

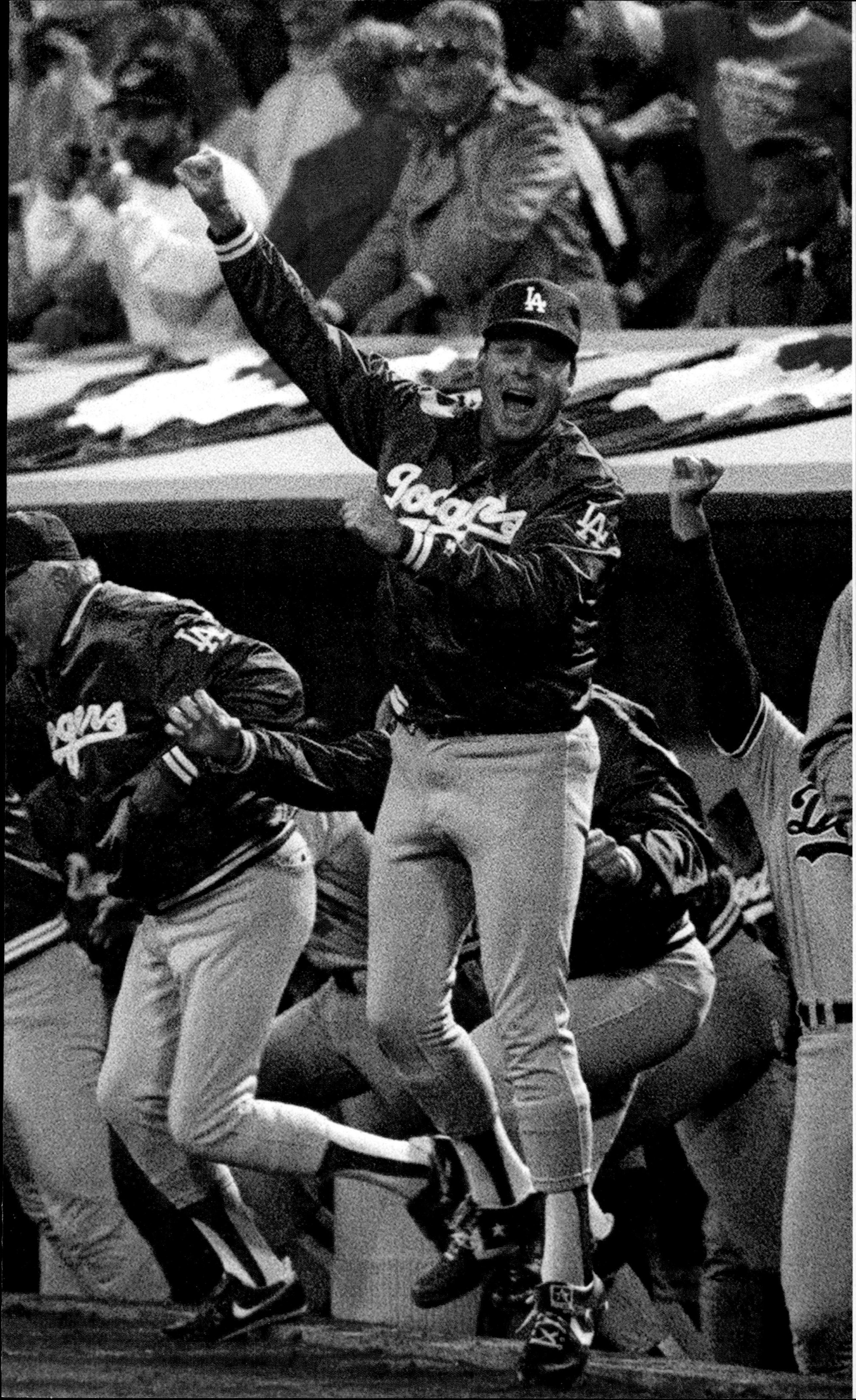

1980s

1980s
Baseball Keeps Growing

1980s Eye of a Tiger
(above) Detroit's Jack Morris won more games than any other Major League pitcher in the 1980s. He had a pair of complete-game triumphs to lead the Tigers past the Padres in the 1984 World Series.

1980 Group hug
(left) Dodgers catcher Rick Dempsey and first baseman Franklin Stubbs (22) greet Orel Hershiser after the pitcher's four-hitter stopped the Oakland A's in the fifth and final game of the 1988 World Series. *(previous pages)* The Dodgers pour out of the dugout to join in the celebration after the final out.

Long-suffering Red Sox fans were poised to celebrate a World Series title in 1986 when the "Curse of the Bambino" struck again. Boston, which has not won a championship since 1918–the Red Sox sold Babe Ruth to the hated Yankees one year later–was one out away from defeating the Mets and winning the '86 Series in six games before disaster struck. Three singles, a wild pitch, and a ground ball that trickled through the legs of first baseman Bill Buckner erased New York's two-run deficit and forced Game 7, which the Mets also won.

But while Buckner, who played 22 seasons and amassed more than 2,700 hits, is unfairly remembered mostly for his gaffe, a number of players are noted for remarkable individual performances in the 1980s.

In 1980, George Brett made a run at becoming baseball's first .400 hitter since Ted Williams in 1941 before finishing at .390. Nolan Ryan pitched his record fifth no-hitter in 1981, and in 1983 became Major League Baseball's all-time strikeout king. Two years later, Pete Rose became its all-time hit leader. And in the 1988 World Series, Kirk Gibson hobbled off the bench to hit one of the most dramatic home runs in baseball history to spark the Dodgers to an upset of the A's in five games.

The eighties closed with a pair of events that shook the baseball world– figuratively and literally.

Figuratively, it was the permanent expulsion of the legendary Rose from the game. Rose was banned in August, 1989, for allegedly betting on baseball.

Literally, it was before Game 3 of the 1989 World Series, when a devastating earthquake struck the San Francisco Bay Area just before the Giants and Oakland A's were to take the field. The 6.9 temblor caused massive damage in the region, though Candlestick Park suffered little harm. Ten days later, the teams returned to the field, and the A's completed a four-game sweep.

465

1980s

1980-81 Oh, Brother
(above) Brothers George Brett–left, who played with the Royals his entire 21-year career–and Ken Brett–who pitched for 10 teams in 14 seasons–were teammates for two years in Kansas City.

1980 Quiz time
(right) Royals reliever Dan Quisenberry led the American League in saves for the first of five times in a six-year span. He had 89 saves over the 1983 and 1984 seasons.

1980s Togetherness
(opposite page) Second baseman Lou Whitaker (front) and shortstop Alan Trammell began the decade in the Tigers' infield, and they ended it there. They formed Detroit's double-play combo for 14 consecutive years.

1980s

1980 Strikeout King

(above) Steve Carlton won 24 games for the Phillies while striking out 286 in 304 innings. He retired following the 1988 season with 329 victories and more strikeouts (4,136) than any other southpaw in history.

1980 Philadelphia story

(right) Mike Schmidt led the National League with 48 home runs and 121 RBI. He played his entire 18-year career for the Phillies, belting 548 home runs and winning 10 Gold Gloves at third base.

1980s Island paradise
(above) Youngsters on Eleuthera Island, Bahamas, take a break from playing ball to pose for a photograph.

1980 The art of catching
(following pages) Hall of Famer Roy Campanella's career was cut short by an automobile accident in 1958, but he continued to tutor Dodgers catchers.

1980 Phillie fanatic
(right) Tug McGraw celebrates the final out of Philadelphia's World Series victory over Kansas City. The umpire does not seem quite as impressed.

1982 Prime-time player

(left) Paul Molitor had a record five
hits in a World Series game for the
Brewers. Molitor, who amassed 3,319
hits in 21 seasons, batted .368 in 29
career postseason games.

1982 The Wizard of Oz

(above) Acrobatic Ozzie Smith's artistry
at shortstop was a key part of St.
Louis' world championship team.
Smith was one of baseball's all-time
great defensive players

1980s

1982 College prospect
(above) That's a youthful-looking
Mark McGwire, who was a promising
pitcher at the University of Southern
California before switching to first
base full-time.

1982 The joys of spring
(right) When you're the defending
champions, you have to work twice
as hard. The Dodgers' Steve Garvey
readies for the 1982 season at spring
training in Vero Beach, Florida.

1982 Ready to run

(left) Oakland outfielder Rickey Henderson recorded a Major League record 130 steals in 149 games. Henderson swiped 100 or more bases in three of four seasons from 1980 to 1983.

1982 And still growing

(above) Little League Baseball began as a small, local boys program. By 1982, nearly 2 million boys and girls around the world played in nearly 7,000 baseball and softball leagues.

1980s

1982 Fountain of youth
(left) Jesse Orosco delivers a pitch in his first full big-league season. Orosco, who would pitch into his forties, made more appearances than any other pitcher in history.

1982 to 1983 Back-to-back
(above) Atlanta's Dale Murphy blistered opposing pitchers for 72 home runs and drove in 230 runs while earning consecutive MVP awards.

485

1983 Rags to riches
(above) The Yankees' Dave Righetti
fires a pitch during a no-hitter over
the Red Sox. "Rags" eventually
would become one of baseball's
best closers.

1983 This one missed
(right) Don Baylor turns out of the
way of a pitch while with the
Yankees. Baylor was plunked 267
times in his 20 seasons, more than
any other player in history.

1980s

1983 Straw Man

(below) Heralded 21-year-old rookie Darryl Strawberry joined the Mets and clubbed 26 home runs. He hit 252 round trippers in eight seasons in New York.

1984 to 1985 The magic number

(right) Joaquin Andujar posted back-to-back 20-win seasons for the Cardinals. His 21 victories in 1985 helped St. Louis win the National League pennant.

1984 to 1985 The joy of victory
(opposite page) Willie Hernandez and Lance Parrish celebrate the Tigers' victory over the Padres in the 1984 World Series. *(above)* Cal State Fullerton players rejoice after beating Texas to win the College World Series in 1984. *(right)* Hal McRae shares some champagne with George Brett after the Royals edged the Cardinals in seven games to win the 1985 World Series.

1984 Good start
(*left*) Don Mattingly broke into the Yankees' regular lineup in 1984 and won the A.L. batting championship with a .343 average. One year later, he was the league's MVP.

1984 Good finish
(*above*) The Angels' Mike Witt delivers a pitch en route to a perfect game over the Texas Rangers. Witt fashioned his gem, the 13th in major-league history, on the final day of the season.

1980s Two of a kind
(above) Eddie Murray (33) and Cal Ripken were mainstays in the Orioles' lineup most of the decade, including 1983, when they helped Baltimore to the world championship.

1984 Post-Olympic career
(right) Peter Ueberroth (second from left), who organized the 1984 Olympic Games in Los Angeles, succeeded Bowie Kuhn as the Commissioner of Baseball.

1984 Role reversal
(left) Veteran Dennis Eckersley joined the Cubs and continued to be an effective starter. It was not until he was traded to Oakland in 1987 that he became one of baseball's all-time great relief pitchers.

1984 A first for the Cubs
(left) Second baseman Ryne Sandberg's MVP season (.304 average, a league-best 114 runs scored and 19 triples) led the Cubs to their first N.L. East title.

1984 Women's movement
(above) Victoria Roche became the first girl to play at the Little League World Series when she participated on a team from Brussels, Belgium.

1980s

1985 Ty breaker
Pete Rose follows through on career hit number 4,192 against San Diego's Eric Show on September 11. With the single, Rose surpassed legendary Ty Cobb as baseball's all-time hit king.

1980s

1985 Bulldog
(above) The Dodgers' Orel Hershiser won 19 of 22 decisions with an ERA of 2.03 while displaying a tenacity that would make him one of the decade's most effective pitchers.

1985 Multiple weapons
(left) Rickey Henderson (far left) led the A.L. with 80 steals and Don Mattingly had a Major League-best 145 RBI, but the Yankees fell two games short of the Blue Jays in the division race.

1985 One-man team
(right) Ryne Sandberg became only the third player in history to steal more than 50 bases (54) and hit more than 25 homers (26) in the same season, but the Cubs slipped to fourth place.

1985 The Kid
(above) After 11 years in Montreal, catcher Gary Carter joined the Mets and hit 32 homers, drove in 100 runs, and earned his seventh consecutive All-Star selection.

1985 King of the Minors
(left) That's Stan Wasiak, who won a record 2,530 games in more than 30 seasons as a manager in the minor leagues.

1986 Friends and enemies
(above) Darryl Strawberry and
Keith Hernandez (17), who
later had a well-publicized
fight during a team photo shoot,
helped fuel the Mets' title run.

1986 Quick study
(right) Davey Johnson, who was a
four-time All-Star second baseman, led the Mets to the World
Series in just his third season as a
Major League manager.

1986 Bo knows baseball
(left) Bo Jackson, college football's
Heisman Trophy winner in 1985,
joined the Kansas City Royals.
By 1989, he was an All-Star
selection.

1980s

1986 Power and speed
(above) Reds' outfielder Eric Davis emerged as a potent threat at the plate or on the bases. He belted 27 home runs and stole 80 bases in his first season as a regular.

1986 New York's finest
(right) Ecstatic members of the New York Mets celebrate after winning the World Series. On the brink of defeat in Game 6, the Mets rallied to beat the Red Sox in seven games.

1986 20 for 21
Roger Clemens walks off the field
after one of his Major League record
20 strikeouts in a 3-1 victory over the
Seattle Mariners.

1986 Competing interests
Red Sox first baseman Bill Buckner
may have been surprised to find
himself battling a Fenway fan who
was trying to grab a souvenir.

1987 Heart of a Giant
(left) Padres Dave Dravecky was traded to San Francisco and helped win a division title before a cancerous tumor in his pitching arm sidelined him a year later.

1987 Home, sweet home
(previous pages) The Twins won all four games played in the Metrodome to edge the Cardinals in seven games and win their first World Series title.

1987 Last and first
(above) The Cubs won only 76 games, but free-agent signee Andre Dawson belted 49 home runs and became the first MVP winner to play on a last-place team.

1980s

1987 Best seats in the house
These Cubs fans are right at home across Chicago's North Sheffield Avenue, in full view of historic Wrigley Field.

515

1980s

1988 What a relief
(above) The Athletics converted starter Dennis Eckersley to closer in 1987, and in 1988 he led the league with 45 saves as Oakland won the pennant. Four years later, he had a career-best 51 saves.

1988 Life imitates art
(right) A player in Durham, North Carolina, tosses a pitch to a youngster. The same year, the city's minor-league team was immortalized in the motion-picture comedy *Bull Durham*.

HIT BULL WIN STEAK
DURHAM
The
Bokshop
CHAPEL HILL
RALEIGH
FAYETTEVILLE
CHARLOTTE

1988 Successful demonstration

(above) Though baseball still was considered a demonstration sport and not granted medal status, the United States won the title at the 1988 Olympics in Seoul. Future Major Leaguer Jim Abbott (34) beat defending-champion Japan in the final.

1988 To the victors

(right) General manager Fred Claire and manager Tommy Lasorda hoist the spoils of the Dodgers' World Series triumph over the Oakland A's: baseball's World Championship Trophy.

1988 What else would they call it?

(left) A reliever warms up for the Durham Bulls of the International League—he's throwing in the bullpen, of course.

1980s

1988 Captain Kirk
Kirk Gibson belts one of the most memorable home runs in baseball history. Leg injuries kept Gibson, the Dodgers' emotional leader and the National League's MVP, out of the lineup for Game 1 of the World Series against Oakland. But he hobbled off the bench with two outs in the bottom of the ninth inning and his team trailing by one run. His two-run blast off Dennis Eckersley gave Los Angeles a 5-4 victory and ignited an upset of the A's. It was Gibson's only at-bat of the Series.

1989 Happy days are here again
(above) Just two years removed from a last-place finish, Chicago Cubs fans celebrate their club's National League Eastern Division championship.

1989 Mr. President
(right) George W. Bush, who would become president of the United States in January, 2001, led an investor group that purchased a controlling interest in the American League's Texas Rangers.

1989 Will the Thrill
(left) First baseman Will Clark rejoices as the final out is recorded in San Francisco's victory over Chicago in the League Championship Series. Clark hit .650 in the five-game series to lead the Giants to their first pennant in 27 years.

1980s

1989 Fifty years young
(above) Little League Baseball celebrated its golden anniversary. The organization was founded by Williamsport, Pennsylvania, resident Carl Stotz in 1939.

1989 Family first
(previous pages) Members of the Oakland A's and their families walk off the field at Candlestick Park after a major earthquake struck the San Francisco Bay Area just moments before the Giants and A's were to begin Game 3 of the World Series.

1989 Just how big leaguers do it
(right) Members of the Trumbull, Connecticut, team celebrate after a 5-2 upset of Taipei, Taiwan, in the final game of the Little League World Series.

1989 Hard to say good-bye
(left) Mike Schmidt, arguably the greatest all-around third baseman in Major League history, wipes away a tear after announcing his retirement early in the season.

1980s

1989 One play, three outs
Umpire Terry Tata makes the call as
Padres catcher Mark Parent holds
his glove aloft after tagging out
the Astros' Kevin Bass. Parent's tag
completed a triple play.

1990s
Back to the Future

1990s The Big Unit
(above) Randy Johnson was one of baseball's dominant pitchers in the nineties. The southpaw intimidated batters with his 6-foot 10-inch frame and an overpowering fastball.

1990s Exclusive club
(left) Outfielder Barry Bonds became the first player in Major League history to win three MVP awards in a four-year span and the first to record 400 career home runs along with 400 steals.

1990s Big Mac
(previous pages) St. Louis slugger Mark McGwire caps an historic 1998 season with his 70th home run on the final day. McGwire shattered Roger Maris' mark of 61 homers in 1961.

Baseball engineered a remarkable comeback in the 1990s, rallying from the depths of a mid-decade work stoppage that tested the loyalties of even its most ardent fans to the heights of one of its most memorable seasons in 1998.

For a while, the sport seemed threatened by the prosperity of the 1990s. Even as salaries continued to escalate to all-time highs for the players and more revenue streams developed for the owners, the growing rift between the two sides threatened baseball's stability.

It all boiled over in 1994, when a player strike ended the season on August 12 and left baseball without a World Series for the first time since 1904.

But any lingering animosity from the labor struggle was set aside during the summer of 1998, when a number of historic individual performances and the Yankees' record 125 victories focused attention squarely on the field. In particular, the Cardinals' Mark McGwire and the Cubs' Sammy Sosa captured the attention of fans and nonfans alike by threatening Roger Maris' single-season home-run record. Each eventually surpassed Maris' 61, with McGwire ending the season at an outrageous 70 and Sosa at 66.

Pre-strike action also was highlighted by a big swing: Joe Carter's three-run home run in the bottom of the ninth inning of Game 6 gave Toronto a World Series victory over Philadelphia in 1993. It was only the second time that a World Series ended with a blast out of the park (after Pittsburgh's Bill Mazeroski in 1960), and it gave the Canadian franchise its second consecutive title.

But by the late nineties, it was an American staple–the Yankees–who returned to prominence. New York won its first World Series in 18 years in 1996, then began a string of three consecutive titles in 1998.

The decade ended with baseball saluting its All-Century team. Lou Gehrig, Babe Ruth, Hank Aaron, Ted Williams, and Willie Mays topped the balloting on the 30-man squad.

1990s

1990-91 Like father, like son
(*above*) Veteran Ken Griffey, Sr., left, and budding superstar Ken Griffey, Jr., played together in the Seattle Mariners' lineup.

1990s A game for everyone
(*right*) Baseball's popularity extended to all ages and both sexes, as women players began appearing at the Little League, high school, and college levels.

1990s Designated Hitter
(*far right*) Seattle's Edgar Martinez batted better than .300 eight times in the nineties, including a whopping .356 in 1995 and .343 in 1992, both A.L. bests.

1990s

1990 Minor praise
(previous pages) Minor-league players take a moment out of their work day in Junction City, Arkansas.

1991 Seventh heaven
(above) Pinch-hitter Gene Larkin's 10th-inning, bases-loaded single drives in Dan Gladden with the only run of Game 7 and lifts the Twins past the Braves in the 1991 World Series.

1991 Grand theft
(right) A's outfielder Rickey Henderson holds third base aloft after his 939th career steal, breaking Lou Brock's previous Major League record.

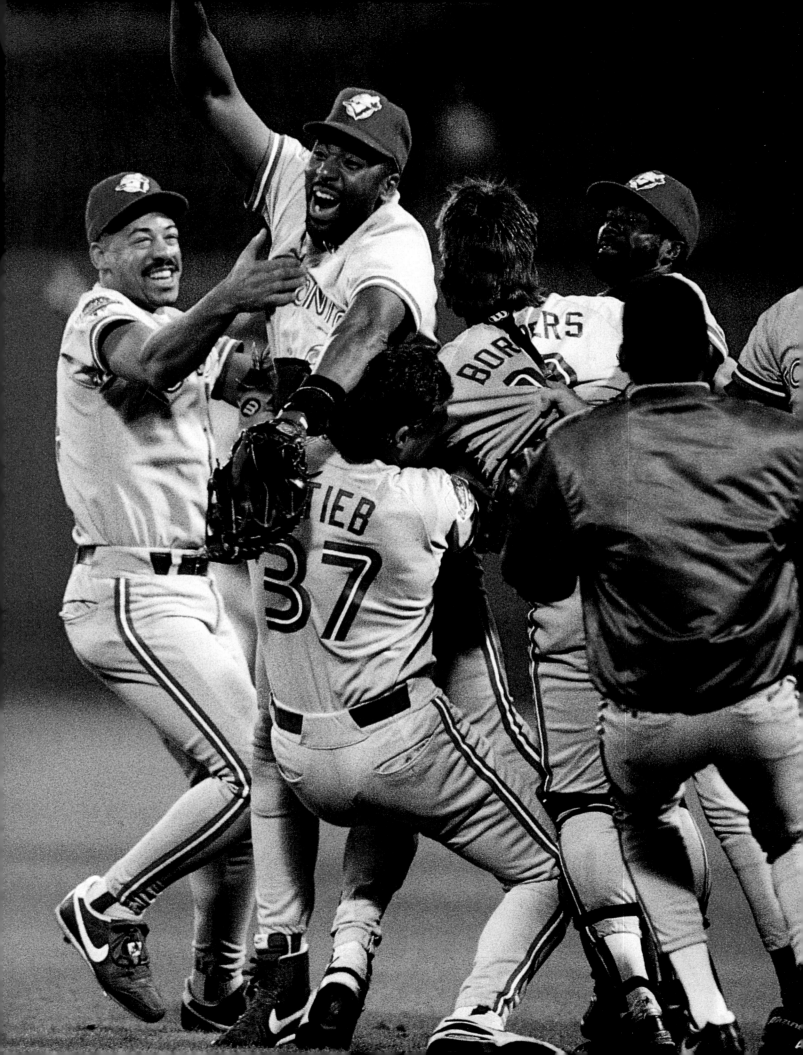

1990s

1992 North of the border
(left) The Blue Jays celebrate after defeating the Braves in six games in the 1992 World Series. Toronto became the first team from outside of the United States to win the Series.

1992 Home protection
(right) Hard-nosed catcher Gary Carter concluded a marvelous 19-year career in which he clubbed 324 home runs and excelled on defense.

1990s True blue
(below) Gregarious skipper Tom Lasorda was one of baseball's most prominent ambassadors. He managed Los Angeles for 20 seasons before stepping down for health reasons in 1996.

1990s

1993 Finishing touch
(above) Toronto's Joe Carter exults as
his ninth-inning home run against
Philadelphia clears the wall in Game 6
of the World Series and gives the Blue
Jays their second consecutive title.

1993 Field of dreams
(right) High school players all over
the country dream of making it to
the big leagues. This one, from
Miami, was a future Major League
star: Alex Rodriguez.

1990s

1993 Goodbye kiss
(above) Kansas City's George Brett kisses home plate after playing the final home game of a 21-year career in which he amassed 3,154 hits and batted .305.

1993 Big Cat
(left) The Colorado Rockies joined the National League as an expansion franchise and revitalized the career of Andres Galarraga, who hit a league-high .370.

1993 Turkish delight
(right) Rookie pitcher Turk Wendell of the Chicago Cubs entertained fans with his quirks, including a leap over the foul line on each trip to and from the mound.

1990s

1993 Ageless Wonder
Forty-six-year-old Nolan Ryan delivers a pitch for the Texas Rangers in his 27th, and final, Major League season.

1990s

1994 Career change
(above) Michael Jordan, best known for his exploits on the hardwood, chases a fly ball for the minor-league Birmingham Barons.

1994 40-40 vision
(right) Jose Canseco takes a mighty swing for the Rangers. Baseball's first 40-homer, 40-steal player joined Texas in 1992 after seven-plus years in Oakland.

1994 Big hitter
(left) After playing the 1989 season in Japan, imposing Cecil Fielder returned to the United States and hit 245 home runs for the Tigers between 1990 amd 1996.

1990s Closing time
(above) Lee Smith led the league in saves three times in the decade. He saved a record 478 games for eight teams in his 18-year career.

1994 Pitcher perfect
Texas' Kenny Rogers is mobbed
by teammates after retiring all 27
batters he faced in a 4-0 victory
over the California Angels.

1990s

1995 Tornado watch
Japan's Hideo Nomo, nicknamed
"Tornado" for his contorted delivery,
took the majors by storm, winning
13 games and striking out 236 in
191 innings.

1995 Good penmanship
Minor-league players get Major
League treatment from young
autograph seekers.

1990s

1995 Blow by blow
(previous pages) Mexico catcher Alberto Vargas tries to blow a ball into foul territory in a game against Guatemala in the Pan American Games.

1995 Call waiting
(above) Members of the Billings Mustangs' bullpen bide their time in the sun during a minor-league game.

1995 Foreign Legion
(left) Former major leaguer Tom O'Malley (center) was the most valuable player of the Yakult Swallows' victory over the Orix Bluewaves in the Japan Series.

1996 Number one
(right) Pitcher John Wetteland shows where the Yankees stand after closing out the Braves in Game 6 of the World Series.

1996 Everybody plays
(left and above) Participants have fun in
Little League Baseball's Challenger Division.
Since 1988, the Challenger Division has
enabled boys and girls, age 5 to 18 to
enjoy baseball, regardless of mental or
physical challenges.

1990s

1996 Passion play

(above) Baseball always has inspired passion from its supporters. These fervent fans helped cheer the Rangers to a division title in 1996.

1996 All's Wells

(right) David Wells won 11 games for Baltimore after signing as a free agent. Wells pitched for six franchises from 1987 to 2001, and helped the 1992 Blue Jays and 1998 Yankees to world titles.

1996 Good as gold
(left) Cuban players celebrate their gold-medal victory in the 1996 Olympics in Atlanta.

1996 Viva Las Vegas
(above) The Oakland Athletics meet one of the local residents at a preseason game in Las Vegas.

1996 Home of the Braves
(left) Greg Maddux anchored a pitching staff that carried Atlanta to the World Series for the fourth time since 1991. The Braves won five National League pennants in the 1990s.

1996 Hero's welcome
(right) The Yankees' Bernie Williams (51) is greeted by teammates at home plate. Williams hit .305 and drove in more than 100 runs to help the Yankees to their first world title since 1978.

1996 to 1999 Power supply
(below) Red Sox shortstop Nomar Garciaparra made his Major League debut in 1996, then hit .326 and averaged 31 home runs and 108 RBI over his first three full seasons.

1996 Amazing grace
(following pages) Shortstop Derek Jeter broke into the Yankees' lineup and won over New Yorkers with his on-field play and his off-field demeanor.

1990s

1997 Switch hitter
Colorado's Larry Walker was the National League's
MVP after hitting 49 homeruns and driving in 130 runs.
But the left-handed batter took no chances in the
All-Star Game, turning to the right side to face hard-
throwing lefty Randy Johnson of the American League.

1997 A time to remember

(above) Baseball commemorated the golden anniversary of the breaking of the color barrier. President Bill Clinton (right) extolled Jackie Robinson in a speech at New York's Shea Stadium.

1990s

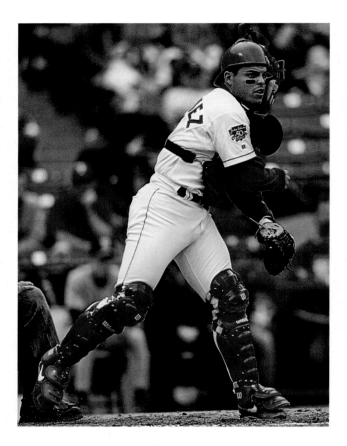

1997 Theft deterrent
Rangers catcher Ivan Rodriguez possesses one of the most powerful and accurate throwing arms in the game. He's a force at the plate as well.

1997 Brown out
(*right*) Marlins pitcher Kevin Brown finishes off a no-hitter against the San Francisco Giants in June. One month later, he tossed a one-hitter against the Dodgers.

1997 Juan Gone

(left) Juan Gonzalez belted 42 home runs and drove in 131 runs—one of his five 40-plus home run and seven 100-plus RBI seasons in the 1990s.

1997 Fish tale

(right) Edgar Renteria's 11th-inning single wins Game 7 against Cleveland and gives the Florida Marlins a World Series title in only the franchise's fifth season.

1998 Holy Cal!

(below) Fans were accustomed to seeing Cal Ripken's name in the Orioles' lineup. In September, 1998, they were stunned to see his record-breaking streak end at 2,632 games.

1998 Coast-to-coast
All-star catcher Mike Piazza, a fan favorite in Los Angeles, was traded from the Dodgers to the Marlins, then to the Mets. He became an all-star in New York, too.

1998 Unhittable
(left) Pedro Martinez, the N.L. Cy Young Award winner in 1997, joined the Red Sox and won 19 games while striking out 251 batters in 234 innings.

1998 Up for grabs
(right) Part of the fun of coming out to the ballpark is trying to catch a foul ball.

1998 Mr. Consistency
(below) Baltimore's Cal Ripken reaches for a ground ball. Ripken is best known for his ironman streak, but he also was one of the best hitting and fielding short-stops throughout the 1990s.

1990s

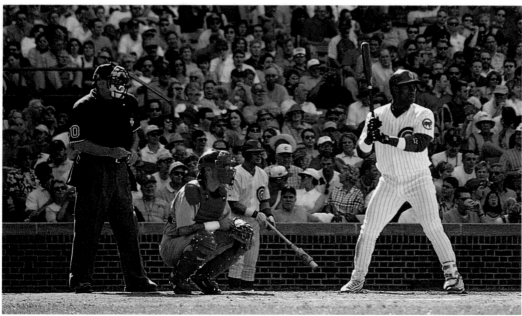

1998 Slammin' Sammy
The Cubs' Sammy Sosa *(above, left,* and *right)* dueled St. Louis' Mark McGwire in a memorable season-long chase of Roger Maris' home run record. Sosa finished the season with 66 homers, second in Major League history only to McGwire's 70 the same season.

1990s

1998 Number 62
(*above*) Cardinals slugger Mark
McGwire hits his record-breaking
62nd home run of the season off the
Cubs' Steve Trachsel on September 9.

1998 Number 70

(above) Mark McGwire hits his
70th, and final, home run of the
year off Montreal's Carl Pavano in
the seventh inning of the season
finale on September 27. At right
is a bird's-eye view of the
historic blast.

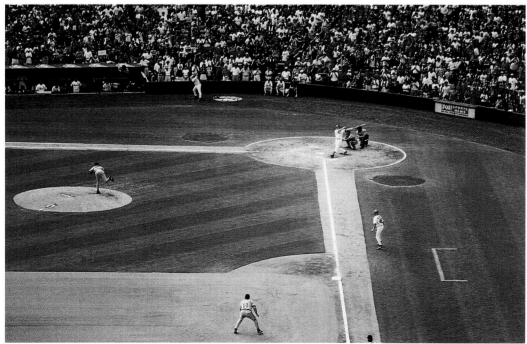

1998 The Big Hurt
(*left*) White Sox slugger Frank Thomas connects. Thomas averaged 33 home runs and 112 RBI in nine full seasons in the 1990s.

1998 Special Ks
(*above*) Twenty-year-old Kerry Wood made an immediate impact his first month in the big leagues, striking out a Major League record-tying 20 batters for the Cubs in a victory over Houston.

1998 A league of her own
(left) Ila Borders became the first woman to win a men's professional game while pitching for the Northern League's Duluth-Superior Dukes.

1998 Perennial All-Star
(left) Second baseman Roberto Alomar made the All-Star team every year during the nineties while playing for four franchises.

1998 Past and present
(right) Cardinals fans out to see star Mark McGwire at Busch Stadium pause at the statue of one of the franchise's all-time greats, Hall of Famer Stan Musial.

1990s

1999 World of opportunity
(right) Little League Baseball programs reach 100 countries throughout the world for the first time. The Little League World Series is held each year in Williamsport, Pennsylvania.

1999 Safeco Field
(left) After playing more than two decades in the Kingdome, the Seattle Mariners moved into a new open-air park (with a retractable roof) in the summer of 1999.

1999 Minor Miracle
(right) Catcher Matthew LeCroy of the Fort Myers Miracle holds his trophy for winning the Florida State League's annual home run hitting contest.

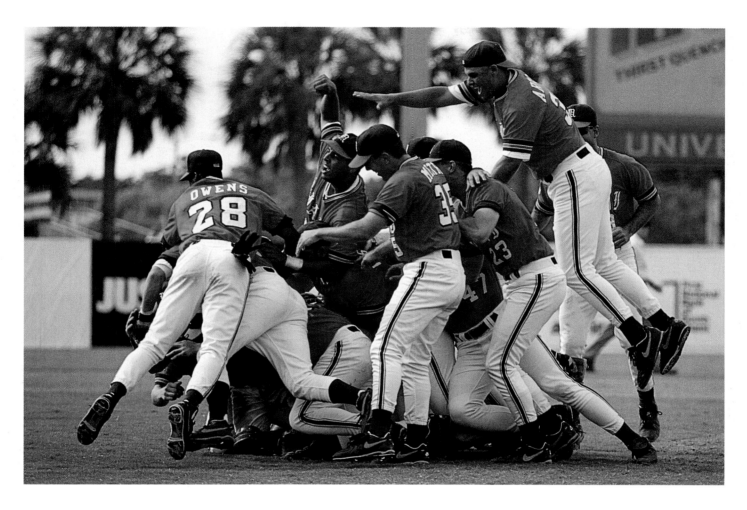

1999 Hurricane warning
(above) Members of the University of Miami baseball team celebrate a regional title en route to the Hurricanes' third NCAA title.

1999 Crossing enemy lines
(left) Roger Clemens, who played 13 of his first 15 seasons with the Red Sox, joined Boston's bitter rivals and helped the Yankees win a World Series.

1999 Hitting Machine
(right) Padres outfielder Tony Gwynn won four National League batting titles in the nineties and stroked his 3,000th hit in August, 1999.

1990s

1999 International flavor
(above) Baseball's popularity has boomed around the world. In 1999, Baltimore played an exhibition against Cuba's national team.

1999 The Old Guard
Despite the boom in young talent in the decade, veteran future Hall of Famers such as Baltimore's Cal Ripken (*right*) still found their place on the field.

1999 The New Guard
(*far right*) Derek Jeter (pictured), Nomar Garciaparra, and Alex Rodriguez were representative of a talent boom at shortstop in the 1990s.

1999 Lefty
(above) The Texas Rangers' Mike Venafro lets loose a pitch.

1999 The Commish
(right) Commissioner Bud Selig oversaw baseball through most of the 1990s and into the new century.

1999 Instant winner
(left) Kevin Brown, who helped carry Florida and San Diego to postseason play the previous two seasons, signed with the Dodgers and won 18 games.

1999 Coming at you
(left) Randy Johnson signed with Arizona as a free agent. He struck out a whopping 364 batters and allowed only 207 hits in 272 innings while winning the Cy Young Award.

1999 Good housekeeping
(right) An umpire meticulously dusts off home plate. Following tradition, umpires always face the stands while performing this task.

1999 Spellbound
(below) High school players watch and wait for their opportunity to take the field.

1990s

1999 Grand-slam single
Robin Ventura watches his bases-loaded blast clear the fence with the score tied 3-3 in the bottom of the 15th inning of Game 5 of the N.L. Championship Series against the Braves. Ventura was credited with a single after he was mobbed by jubilant teammates on the basepaths.

1990s

1999 Bleacher bums
(above) There's still nothing quite as good as a day at the park, especially for these fans sitting in the bleachers at Wrigley Field.

1999 Yankee skipper
(left) Manager Joe Torre guided the Yankees to back-to-back World Series titles to close the decade.

1999 Victory ride
(right) New York's David Cone is carried off the field after pitching a perfect game against the Montreal Expos at Yankee Stadium.

2000s
A New Millennium

2000s

2000 They got five

(above) New Yorkers were rewarded with a World Series between the Yankees and Mets, though it took the American Leaguers only five games to dispatch the N.L. champs.

2000 No apparent weaknesses

(left) Shortstop Alex Rodriguez was one of baseball's brightest young stars entering the new decade. A multifaceted player who can hit, field, run, and throw well, Rodriguez left Seattle for Texas via free agency in 2001.

2000 Around the world

(previous pages) Pregame ceremonies before the Mets and Cubs opened baseball's regular season in Tokyo, Japan.

As the world increasingly became a global community at the turn of the century, it was only fitting that Major League Baseball opened its regular season outside of North America for the first time in 2000: The New York Mets and the Chicago Cubs began the year with a two-game series in Tokyo, Japan.

Major league rosters were dotted with more and more players from around the world as well. Latin American players had long made an impact on the big leagues, and now they were joined by players from places such as Asia and Australia as well.

Japan's Kazuhiro Sasaki led the American League West-champion Mariners with 37 saves in 2000, and a year later, Seattle signed outfielder Ichiro Suzuki. Another native of Japan, veteran Hideo Nomo, fashioned his second career no-hitter while pitching for the Red Sox early in the 2001 season.

By Opening Day that year, more than a quarter of all major league players hailed from outside the United States. They represented the Dominican Republic, Puerto Rico, Venezuela, Mexico, Canada, Cuba, Panama, Japan, Australia, Colombia, Nicaragua, Korea, England, Jamaica, the U.S. Virgin Islands, Aruba, and Curaçao.

But even as baseball grew internationally, the United States reminded the world that it is still a uniquely American game when Tom Lasorda's squad captured its first official Olympic gold medal in 2000 by defeating Cuba in the title game in Australia.

On the home front, baseball entered a new millennium boasting a host of marquee players still at the top of their game, rising young stars, and robust attendance.

And the new century picked up right where the old one left off, with the Yankees winning the World Series yet again in 2000.

This time, New York withstood a challenge from its intracity rival, the Mets, taking five games to win the first Subway Series since 1956.

607

2000s

2000 Fan friendly
(above) Buoyed by new stadiums, exciting races, and emerging stars, Major League baseball drew more than 72.7 million fans, a new single-season record.

2000 Subway Series
(left) The Yankees-Mets World Series was the first "Subway Series" since the Yankees beat the Brooklyn Dodgers in seven games in 1956.

2000 Piazza delivers
(right) Mike Piazza helped power the Mets to their first pennant since 1986. The All-Star catcher hit .324, blasted 38 home runs, and drove in 113 runs.

2000 New York, New York

(above) The New York Yankees and the New York Mets line up for introductions prior to the start of the World Series at Yankee Stadium.

2000 Boston pop

(right) Nomar Garciaparra gives the Red Sox a shortstop who can hit. He won his second consecutive batting title (with a .372 average), while hitting 21 homers and driving in 96 runs.

2000 Red Menace

(left) Ken Griffey, Jr., a 10-time All-Star in the American League, joined the Cincinnati Reds and slugged 40 home runs in his first year in the National League.

2000s

2000 Friendly rivalry
(left) The Phillie Phanatic playfully takes exception to the New York Mets' hat donned by this 9-year-old in Palmer Township, Pennsylvania.

2000 They dig the long ball
(right) Home runs are cause for celebration at any level, especially for these youngsters awaiting a slugger's arrival at home plate in the Little League World Series.

2000 Is it my turn yet?
(below) Young players wait for their chance to show off hitting skills at an annual summer baseball camp in Lufkin, Texas.

2000s

2000 Out at home
(above) A close play at the plate in the Little League World Series. The Bellaire, Texas, catcher tagged out the runner from Vancouver, Washington.

2000 Go for the gold
(following pages) Players from the U.S. team pose with their gold medals from the 2000 Olympic Games in Australia. It was the first gold medal victory for the United States in baseball, which officially became an Olympic sport in 1992.

2000 Title insurance
(right) Six-time All-Star Jose Canseco was acquired by the Yankees and helped with their late-season pennant drive, but one year later he was released by the Angels in spring training.

2000 Second to none
(left) National League MVP Jeff Kent drove in 475 runs from 1997 to 2000—more than any other second baseman over a four-year period in baseball history.

2000 Baseball on parade
(right) It's opening day for youth baseball in Brooklyn, where three teammates take part in the annual parade that marks the day.

2000 Prep work
(below) A player from champion LaPorte High School eludes the tag in the state class 4A title game against Evansville Harrison in Indianapolis, Indiana.

2000s

2000 Road to Rio
(left) Little League players line up to greet their opponents in Rio de Janeiro. Brazil became the 104th country around the world with a Little League program.

2000 Diamonds are forever
(above) For Tracye Taylor and Joe
Menges, who were wed at Cy Young
Memorial Park in Newcomerstown,
Ohio, home (plate) is where the heart is.

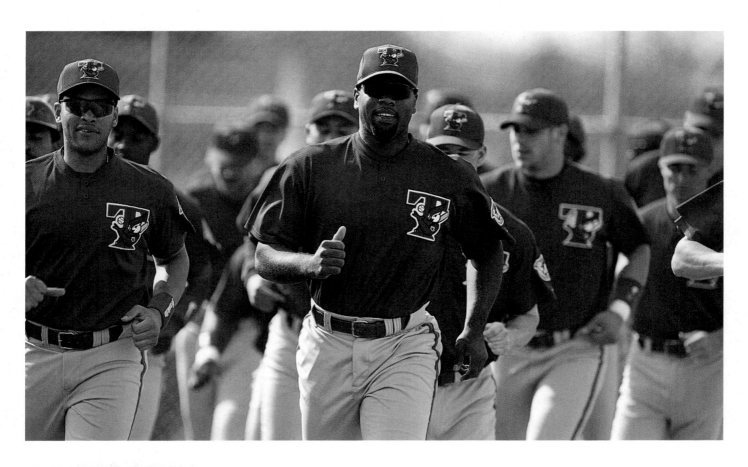

2001 Rites of spring
(above) Carlos Delgado (center) and his Blue Jays teammates loosen up prior to the start of spring drills in Dunedin, Florida.

2001 Nomo's No-No
(left) Catcher Jason Varitek is the first to greet Hideo Nomo after the Boston hurler pitched a no-hitter against the Orioles the first week of the season.

2001 Father's Day
(right) Giants outfielder Barry Bonds and his dad, Bobby, a former Major League star, embrace after the younger Bonds hit career home run number 500 against the Dodgers in April.

Photography Credits

Note: All images listed as "National Baseball Library" were supplied by the National Baseball Hall of Fame and Library Archives through the offices of Major League Baseball Photos. Every effort was made to provide accurate credits for each photograph; however, any errors of credit will be corrected with our apologies in future editions of this work.

Introduction
6-8	AP/Wide World; Author's collection
8-9	Mike Eliason; Author's collection
10-11	National Baseball Library; Corbis/Bettman
12-13	National Baseball Library

"Photographic Memories"
14-15	Rich Pilling/MLB Photos; Jayne Kamin-Oncea
16-17	National Baseball Library (2)
18-19	Rich Pilling/MLB Photos
20-21	AP/Wide World (2)
22-23	National Baseball Library; AP/Wide World
24-25	National Baseball Library; John Williamson/MLB Photos

Early Days (1845-75)
26-27	Transcendental Graphics
28-29	Transcendental Graphics; National Baseball Library (2)
30-31	Brooklyn Public Library; Transcendental Graphics (2); National Baseball Library
32-33	Transcendental Graphics; Library of Congress
34-35	National Baseball Library; Library of Congress/Matthew Brady
36-37	National Baseball Library (2)

The Game Grows (1876-99)
38-39	Transcendental Graphics
40-41	National Baseball Library (2)
42-43	National Baseball Library (2)
44-45	National Baseball Library (2)
46-47	National Baseball Library (2)
48-49	National Baseball Library (2)
50-51	Cleveland Public Library
52-53	National Baseball Library
54-55	National Baseball Library (2)
56-57	National Baseball Library; Library of Congress
58-59	Library of Congress

The Major Leagues Are Born (1900-1909)
60-61	National Baseball Library
62-63	National Baseball Library (2)
64-65	National Baseball Library
66-67	Cleveland Public Library; Library of Congress
68-69	Transcendental Graphics; National Baseball Library
70-71	Library of Congress (top); National Baseball Library (2)
72-73	AP/Wide World; Cleveland Public Library; National Baseball Library
74-75	National Baseball Library (2)
76-77	Collection of Bill Pintard
78-79	Transcendental Graphics; National Baseball Library
80-81	National Baseball Library (2)
82-83	Transcendental Graphics
84-85	National Baseball Library (2)
86-87	Courtesy Alaska Bucs Baseball Team
88-89	National Baseball Library (2)
90-91	AP/Wide World; Library of Congress

High Hopes and Black Sox (1910-1919)
92-93	Virginia Historical Society
94-95	Corbis/Bettman; National Baseball Library
96-97	National Baseball Library (2)
98-99	National Baseball Library (2)
100-101	National Baseball Library
102-103	Transcendental Graphics; National Baseball Library
104-105	National Baseball Library (2)
106-107	National Baseball Library
108-109	Library of Congress (top 108 and 109); National Baseball Library
110-111	National Baseball Library
112-113	National Baseball Library (2)
114-115	National Baseball Library
116-117	National Baseball Library (2)
118-119	National Baseball Library (2); Transcendental Graphics (top)
120-121	Library of Congress (2); National Baseball Library
122-123	National Baseball Library (3)

The Golden Age (1920-1929)
124-125	National Baseball Library
126-127	National Baseball Library (2)
128-129	National Baseball Library (2)

130-131	National Baseball Library
132-133	Transcendental Graphics (2); National Baseball Library (bottom)
134-135	National Baseball Library; Transcendental Graphics
136-137	Transcendental Graphics (3)
138-139	Transcendental Graphics
140-141	National Baseball Library (2)
142-143	Transcendental Graphics
144-145	National Baseball Library (3)
146-147	National Baseball Library
148-149	Library of Congress (top); National Baseball Library(2)
150-151	National Baseball Library; Library of Congress
152-153	Library of Congress; National Baseball Library
154-155	National Baseball Library; Transcendental Graphics
156-157	National Baseball Library (2)
158-159	National Baseball Library
160-161	National Baseball Library (3)
162-163	AP/Wide World; National Baseball Library
164-165	National Baseball Library
166-167	National Baseball Library

The Yankee Years (1930-1939)

168-169	Library of Congress
170-171	AP/Wide World (2)
172-173	AP/Wide World (2)
174-175	AP/Wide World
176-177	AP/Wide World (2)
178-179	AP/Wide World
180-181	AP/Wide World (3)
182-183	AP/Wide World
184-185	AP/Wide World (2)
186-187	AP/Wide World
188-189	AP/Wide World (2)
190-191	AP/Wide World (2)
192-193	AP/Wide World
194-195	AP/Wide World
196-197	AP/Wide World (2)
198-199	Library of Congress/FSA
200-201	AP/Wide World
202-203	AP/Wide World (2)
204-205	Transcendental Graphics; AP/Wide World
206-207	AP/Wide World
208-209	National Baseball Library (2)
210-211	AP/Wide World (2)
212-213	AP/Wide World; National Baseball Library
214-215	Library of Congress/FSA (2)
216-217	National Baseball Library (2)
218-219	National Baseball Library

World War II and Baseball (1940-1949)

220-221	National Baseball Library
222-223	AP/Wide World; National Baseball Library
224-225	Transcendental Graphics
226-227	AP/Wide World
228-229	AP/Wide World
230-231	AP/Wide World; Library of Congress
232-233	Library of Congress/FSA
234-235	AP/Wide World
236-237	Library of Congress/FSA; Transcendental Graphics (top), Library of Congress (bottom)
238-239	AP/Wide World
240-241	Transcendental Graphics; NBL/The Sporting News
242-243	AP/Wide World (2)
244-245	AP/Wide World; National Baseball Library
246-247	AP/Wide World (2)
248-249	AP/Wide World
250-251	AP/Wide World (2)
252-253	AP/Wide World (2)
254-255	AP/Wide World
256-257	AP/Wide World
258-259	AP/Wide World
260-261	Nate Fein/AP/Wide World
262-263	National Baseball Library; AP/Wide World
264-265	Library of Congress; Transcendental Graphics
266-267	AP/Wide World
268-269	AP/Wide World
270-271	National Baseball Library

New York, New York (1950-1959)

272-273	Transcendental Graphics
274-275	AP/Wide World (2)
276-277	AP/Wide World
278-279	AP/Wide World
280-281	AP/Wide World (2)
282-283	AP/Wide World (2); National Baseball Library
284-285	AP/Wide World (3)
286-287	AP/Wide World
288-289	AP/Wide World (2)
290-291	AP/Wide World (2)
292-293	AP/Wide World
294-295	AP/Wide World
296-297	AP/Wide World (2)
298-299	Transcendental Graphics; AP/Wide World; Corbis/Bettman
300-301	AP/Wide World
302-303	AP/Wide World
304-305	AP/Wide World (2)
306-307	AP/Wide World (2)
308-309	National Baseball Library; AP/Wide World
310-311	AP/Wide World (2)

312-313	AP/Wide World
314-315	AP/Wide World
316-317	AP/Wide World; National Baseball Library;
318-319	AP/Wide World
320-321	National Baseball Library/Ernie Sisto
322-323	AP/Wide World (3)
324-325	AP/Wide World
326-327	AP/Wide World (2)
328-329	AP/Wide World (2)
330-331	AP/Wide World (2)
332-333	Corbis/Bettman; National Baseball Library
334-335	AP/Wide World
336-337	AP/Wide World (2)
338-339	Corbis/Bettman; AP/Wide World
340-341	National Baseball Library
342-343	National Baseball Library; AP/Wide World; Corbis/Bettman

Suddenly the Sixties (1960-1969)

344-345	AP/Wide World
346-347	AP/Wide World (2)
348-249	Corbis/Bettman; AP/Wide World
350-351	AP/Wide World; MLB/Photofile
352-353	MLB/Photofile; Corbis/Bettman
354-355	AP/Wide World
356-357	AP/Wide World (2)
358-359	MLB/Photofile; Corbis/Bettman
360-361	AP/Wide World (2)
362-363	Corbis/Bettman (2)
364-365	AP/Wide World
366-367	Corbis/Bettman;AP/Wide World
368-369	AP/Wide World (2)
370-371	Transcendental Graphics
372-373	Corbis/Bettman; AP/Wide World
374-375	Corbis/Bettman
376-377	National Baseball Library; Corbis/Bettman
378-379	AP/Wide World (2)
380-381	AP/Wide World (2)
382-383	AP/Wide World (2)
384-385	Corbis/Bettman (2)
386-387	Corbis/Bettman
388-389	Corbis/Bettman; MLB Photos
390-391	AP/Wide World; Corbis/Bettman
392-393	Corbis/Bettman; AP/Wide World
394-395	Corbis/Bettman; AP/Wide World
396-397	MLB/Photofile; AP/Wide World
398-399	MLB/Photofile; Corbis/Bettman (bottom); AP/Wide World
400-401	Corbis/Bettman (2)
402-403	Corbis/Bettman (2); MLB Photos
404-405	National Baseball Library; Corbis/Bettman

The Polyester Seventies (1970-1979)

406-407	Corbis/Bettman
408-409	MLB Photos (2)
410-411	AP/Wide World; Rich Pilling/MLB Photos
412-413	MLB Photos (3)
414-415	AP/Wide World
416-417	MLB Photos; Rich Pilling/MLB Photos
418-419	MLB Photos (2)
420-421	Corbis/Bettman; Tony Tomsic/MLB Photos
422-423	AP/Wide World
424-425	Tony Tomsic/MLB Photos; AP/Wide World
426-427	MLB Photos (3)
428-429	AP/Wide World
430-431	Fred Kaplan/MLB Photos (left); Rich Pilling/MLB Photos; MLB Photos
432-433	AP/Wide World (2)
434-435	AP/Wide World
436-437	Rich Pilling/MLB Photos (2); Tony Tomsic/MLB Photos
438-439	Corbis/Bettman; Tony Tomsic/MLB Photos; AP/Wide World
440-441	AP/Wide World
442-443	MLB Photos; Rich Pilling/MLB Photos
444-445	MLB Photos; Rich Pilling/MLB Photos
446-447	Corbis/Bettman (2); Rich Pilling/MLB Photos
448-449	AP/Wide World; Rich Pilling/MLB Photos
450-451	Corbis/Bettman; Rich Pilling/MLB Photos; Tony Tomsic/MLB Photos
452-453	AP/Wide World; Corbis/Bettman
454-455	Corbis/Bettman; Rich Pilling/MLB Photos
456-457	Corbis/Bettman; Rich Pilling/MLB Photos (2)
458-459	Corbis/Bettman; Rich Pilling/MLB Photos (2)
460-461	AP/Wide World (2)

Baseball Keeps Growing (1980-1989)

462-463	Jayne Kamin-Oncea
464-465	Rich Pilling/MLB Photos; Jayne Kamin-Oncea
466-467	Rich Pilling/MLB Photos (3)
468-469	Rich Pilling/MLB Photos (2)
470-471	Corbis/Bettman; AP/Wide World
472-473	Corbis/Bettman
474-475	Rich Pilling/MLB Photos (2); Corbis/Bettman (bottom)
476-477	Rich Pilling/MLB Photos (3)
478-479	Rich Pilling/MLB Photos (2)
480-481	University of Southern California; Jayne Kamin-Oncea
482-483	Rich Pilling/MLB Photos; Corbis/Bettman
484-485	Rich Pilling/MLB Photos (2)
486-487	AP/Wide World; Rich Pilling/MLB Photos
488-489	Rich Pilling/MLB Photos (2)

490-491   AP/Wide World (2); Al Messerschmidt (bottom)

492-493   Rich Pilling/MLB Photos; AP/Wide World

494-495   Rich Pilling/MLB Photos (3)

496-497   Rich Pilling/MLB Photos; Little League Baseball

498-499   Rich Pilling/MLB Photos

500-501   Rich Pilling/MLB Photos (2); Bill Livingston/MLB Photos

502-503   Corbis/Bettman; Rich Pilling/MLB Photos

504-505   ASG/MLB Photos; Rich Pilling/MLB Photos (2)

506-507   MLB Photos; Rich Pilling/MLB Photos

508-509   AP/Wide World (2)

510-511   Rich Pilling/MLB Photos

512-513   Rich Pilling/MLB Photos; Tony Tomsic/MLB Photos

514-515   Corbis/Bettman

516-517   Brad Mangin/MLB Photos; Corbis/Bettman

518-519   Corbis/Bettman (2); AP/Wide World

520-521   Rich Pilling/MLB Photos

522-523   AP/Wide World (3)

524-525   Rich Pilling/MLB Photos

526-527   Little League Baseball; AP/Wide World (2)

528-529   AP/Wide World

Back to the Future (1990-1999)

530-531   Ronald Hickman/MLB Photos

532-533   John Reid III/MLB Photos; MLB Photos

534-535   AP/Wide World (top); Little League Baseball; Ben Van Houten/MLB Photos

536-537   Corbis/Bettman

538-539   MLB Photos; Michael Zagaris/MLB Photos

540-541   MLB Photos; Al Messerschmidt; Jon Soohoo/MLB Photos

542-543   MLB Photos; Al Messerschmidt

544-545   AP/Wide World (2); Bob Rosato/MLB Photos

546-547   AP/Wide World

548-549   AP/Wide World; Rich Pilling/MLB Photos

550-551   Rich Pilling/MLB Photos; Don Smith/MLB Photos

552-553   David Woo/MLB Photos

554-555   Jayne Kamin-Oncea; Corbis/Bettman

556-557   AP/Wide World

558-559   Corbis/Bettman (top); AP/Wide World; John Reid III/MLB Photos

560-561   Bill Polo/MLB Photos; David L. Greene/MLB Photos; Rich Pilling/MLB Photos

562-563   Little League Baseball (2)

564-565   Darren Carroll/MLB Photos; Rich Pilling/MLB Photos

566-567   AP/Wide World (2)

568-569   Rich Pilling/MLB Photos; Allen Kee/MLB Photos; John Williamson/MLB Photos

570-571   Rich Pilling/MLB Photos

572-573   Rich Pilling/MLB Photos (3)

574-575   John Williamson/MLB Photos; Michael Zagaris/MLB Photos

576-577   John Williamson/MLB Photos; Rich Pilling/MLB Photos; Michael Zagaris/MLB Photos

578-579   Allen Kee/MLB Photos; Stephen Green/MLB Photos

580-581   Allen Kee/MLB Photos; Mike Eliason; Brad Mangin/MLB Photos

582-583   Stephen Green/MLB (2); Al Messerschmidt (bottom)

584-585   Ron Vesely/MLB Photos; Rich Pilling/MLB Photos; Tim Sater/MLB Photos

586-587   MLB Photos; Ron Vesely/MLB Photos

588-589   Corbis/Bettman; Al Messerschmidt; Allen Kee/MLB Photos (left)

590-591   AP/Wide World; MLB Photos (bottom); Al Messerschmidt

592-593   Al Messerschmidt (top) Kevin Locke/MLB Photos; John Williamson/MLB Photos

594-595   Rich Pilling/MLB Photos (2); John Williamson/MLB Photos

596-597   Rob Shanahan/MLB Photos; Al Messerschmidt; Rich Pilling/MLB Photos

598-599   AP/Wide World (bottom); Rob Shanahan/MLB Photos; Al Messerschmidt

600-601   Rich Pilling/MLB Photos

602-603   Stephen Green/MLB Photos (2); David Seelig/MLB Photos

A New Millennium (2000-2001)

604-605   MLB Photos

606-607   John Reid III/MLB Photos; Brad Mangin/MLB Photos

608-609   MLB Photos; Brad Mangin/MLB Photos; Al Messerschmidt

610-611   Rich Pilling/MLB Photos (3)

612-613   AP/Wide World (3)

614-615   AP/Wide World; Brad Mangin/MLB Photos

616-617   AP/Wide World

618-619   Allen Kee/MLB Photos; AP/Wide World (2)

620-621   AP/Wide World (2)

622-623   Al Messerschmidt; AP/Wide World; SF Giants/Kuno/MLB Photos

Index

D

Acknowledgments

For Patty, Conor, and Katie: My other kinds of "Celebration," and for the Wheezers, who know who they are.-J.B.

For Wendy, Dante, Sophia, Mom and Dad–and for Uncle Joe, who took me to my first big-league game in 1968.-J.G.

————)(————

AUTHORS' ACKNOWLEDGMENTS
The authors would like to thank the many people without whose assistance, expertise, and patience this book would not have been possible.

Don Hintze of Major League Baseball Properties was helpful in putting together the entire package. Rich Pilling and Paul Cunningham of Major League Baseball Photos were absolutely invaluable; they combed the depths of their library in New York, while also paying several visits to the National Baseball Hall of Fame and Library in Cooperstown to pore over literally thousands of photographs to help gather the materials used in this book. Thanks, too, to Bill Burdick of the Hall of Fame for his important assistance in gathering and reproducing the materials from the Hall's incredible collection.

Among photo agencies, Joan Carroll at AP/Wide World helped us dig into that organization's vast collection, while Hanna Edwards was our guide at Corbis/Bettman. Mark Rucker at Transcendental Graphics truly has plumbed the depths of baseball's oldest photography, and this book benefits.

As photographers Al Messerschmidt, Mike Eliason, Rich Pilling, and Jayne Kamin Oncea were also contributors. The Cleveland Public Library and the Brooklyn Public Library were among several institutions who graciously allowed their photos to be included.

Thanks also to Dave Tuttle of the Los Angeles Dodgers publicity staff, who patiently fielded numerous inquiries.

The authors dug into the depths of numerous reference sources for the caption materials, but, as always, any errors of fact are the mistakes of the miners, not the mines. Among this treasure trove were the sixth and seventh editions of *Total Baseball* (Total Sports, 1999 and 2001); many issues of *The Sporting News*; *The Ballplayers* (Arbor House, 1990); *The Baseball Timeline* (DK, 2001); *Baseball's Golden Age: The Photographs of Charles M. Conlon* (Abrams, 1993); *The World Series* (Sporting News, 1991); *Baseball: An Illustrated History* (Alfred A. Knopf, 1994); *The Negro Baseball Leagues: A Photographic History* (Amereon House, 1992); *Baseball: 100 Classic Moments* (DK, 2000); and, finally, the extensive baseball literature collection at the Los Angeles Central Library.

From DK Publishing, special thanks to editors Crystal Coble and Chuck Wills for shepherding the project along track faster than Rickey Henderson in his prime; art editor Megan Clayton for putting up with all of this with more good humor than perhaps should be legal; Jonathan Bennett for his near-constant scanning work; and Sean Moore, for getting it all started in the first place.

Finally, a very special thanks to designer Diana Catherines. She was like the pinch-hitter who comes to the plate with the bases loaded in the bottom of the ninth and her team down by three runs. Even coming in cold, she nevertheless drove a high, hard one deep into the leftfield seats to make our team a winner.

PUBLISHER'S ACKNOWLEDGMENTS
The publishers wish to extend special thanks to Megan Clayton for the many occasions on which her workday went into extra innings on this book. Her skill, hard work, and dedication are much appreciated.